Ya Gotta Wanna Winning
Takes Teamwork

By Malcolm Paice

First published by Creative Book Publishers 01/10/05

Second Edition by Creative Books 03/01/2017
ISBN: 0-978-1-365-76337-3(Paperback) ISBN: 0-978-1-365-76337-3 (Dust Jacket) This book is printed on acid free paper.

You Gotta Wanna

Winning Takes Teamwork

ACKNOWLEDGEMENTS

I would like to thank all the people that read this book as it progressed and provided valuable insight and feedback.

A particular thank-you to Dr. Joel Robertson, who encouraged me, a complete stranger, to put my thoughts on paper during a chance meeting when he couldn't get away from me on a long flight through Chicago.

My friends and family, who patiently waited for me to finish this work, before hearing me converse with them again.

This book is dedicated to Juliana

TABLE OF CONTENTS

FIRST HALF

FOREWORD

As an author of earlier books on performance enhancement and as a consultant to many Fortune 100 companies, I am approached on a weekly basis by someone who claims to have a great book. I normally inform them that there are two criteria I would like to see before I would ever consider looking at their idea. First, they need to be an expert in the field in which they are writing and, secondly, need a new idea or fresh look at a solution. As you can imagine, this limits my "look" to one or two a year.

One day on a flight, I happened to sit next to Malcolm Paice. We were discussing some of my work in brain chemistry and performance when he shared with me his model described in YaGottaWanna. I was more than fascinated, I felt here was a practical, easy-to-use, yet profound model that could be applied to any size company in any arena. I encouraged him to write the book.

When I received the manuscript, I was thrilled to see Malcolm's spoken idea skillfully written in understandable terms.

The model that follows is a profound model that will provide a practical method for any manager to look at his people differently.

I have found in most companies that skill, attitude and personality to reach the company's goals are most often present in the workforce. The voice in the management doesn't know how to utilize their skills. An attitude of discontent and a lack of fulfillment develop among the team members. Productivity decreases, performance drastically changes and poor decision-making ensues. By working within our natural environment with optimal brain chemistry, productivity and joy can replace the negativity and complaining among our team members. In YaGottaWanna, Malcolm provides the framework of the right person in the right place at the right time.

This book is refreshing, fun and so valuable for corporate America, where efficiency, productivity and job satisfaction are key to compete in a global market. I will recommend this book as a must-read for all my friends in management and company executives.

Thank you, Malcolm, for your insights, expertise and practicality in a world of theories without application.

Dr. Joel C. Robertson President and Founder Robertson Research Institute Author - Help Yourself Series of Books and Tapes Natural Prozac

Peak Performance Living

INTRODUCTION

I have spent most of my adult life looking to fix things that are not broken. I love to look at the humorous side of things, and some would say I am too idealistic. I have struggled to find support for the occasional good idea I have had, but I will always be grateful to Dr. Joel Robertson who, during a chance meeting, gave me the moral boost I needed to put pen to paper, or rather, fingers to keyboard.

In his book, The Tipping Point Malcolm Gladwell eloquently describes how changes occur. He writes that great things do not happen without there first being a 'tipping point.' Great changes that have revolutionized methods and approaches to thinking; new products that the market has long been begging for occur after someone, or something, of sufficient importance to influence people's thinking has come on the scene. Gladwell asks, "What rock star has not influenced a million teenagers? What great sports personality has not sold a million products?" They become a tipping point for many of their fans.

Ken Blanchard once said, "None of us is as important as all of us." I have reflected on that for almost as many years as the saying has rattled around in my head, and at the front lines of my imagination. However, what does that mean in practice? To me it means that if we do as Stephen Covey has said – "Begin with the end in mind" – then the important thing is the result. How we get there and who helps (or doesn't help, but still gets some credit) has to be factored in as we attempt to reach the goal, the objective, the dream, the result.

If a goal, the result, is what matters most, then surely getting the right people to take part is crucial. Rarely has anything great been achieved by a person operating in a vacuum. It is a funny thing, but it seems to me the best managers have the knack of surrounding themselves with the right people. Poor managers are oblivious to the people around them, and average managers surround themselves with people just like themselves. However, the best managers create a synergy of players that all buy into the desired result.

As I reflected upon this, I thought about the power of a team. In this sense, who has the hardest job in the world of teams? There is no doubt in my mind that the most difficult job is a sports coach or manager. I happen to love the sport of football (AKA soccer). The team I have followed from my young days has struggled for many years but has always been in the top flight. It has had many managers over the years; all of them promising wonderful things, but only a handful of them have been able to deliver.

Each of these managers came in different sizes and shapes. Each of them had a different philosophy on how the game should be played. All of them had played the beautiful game, and their position on the field of play, more often than not, influenced their focus as a manager years later. For example, a striker like Kevin Keegan could be forgiven for focusing on the fact that a team cannot win if it does not score the most goals. Clearly he knows what he is talking about when it comes to scoring goals. However, a defender, like George Graham, may take the view that a team that has a solid defense and is impenetrable is hard to beat. Perhaps both philosophies are right.

This game plan is not just about winning or losing, in the above sense, it is about the balance that successful managers create in their team. It is about ensuring the players are playing in their best location on the field of play. It is about determining which of those players are versatile enough to play the game just as well, in various positions, at a moment's notice and as circumstances require.

Experienced leaders, rookie managers, or supervisors can use this book alike, as could parents or social groups; in fact, anybody that is concerned with the cohesion of a team will benefit from this material. However, the main target is those for whom a successful team is the only method of success in the workplace — the people concerned with taking a group of individuals and forging them into a team.

THE METAPHOR

Bob Catterick was a highly successful manager. His was the world of sports where he plied his trade as the head coach of his national soccer team. He had spent his apprenticeship learning from some of the greatest managers in the game. He was known for his coaching skills and ability to motivate his players. This was not an easy skill to acquire, because, invariably, he was dealing with a group of men with very shallow egos. Some of that was just because they were men, but the rest of it because it is a typical personality type for professional sports.

Nobody equaled his skill in how to explain to a player that he would not be playing in a particular game, and have him or her feel as if they had just been told they would be. This was not a skill easily learned, but Bob Catterick certainly had it.

However, this was not his greatest trait. His greatest trait was in knowing which players to play, from his squad of talented individuals, for each game. He always knew his opposition and made decisions on which players would be the best in each situation.

His decision on players was also driven by the formation needed for a particular game. For example, if he were playing a traditional 4-4-2, then he would be looking for the best four defenders available to him, the best four midfielders, and the best two strikers. Defining the "best" was not just down to individual skill, for Catterick was never afraid to dip into the pool of players that may not be so technically competent. He would rather have players that understood the concept of teamwork than put an individual on his team who was interested only in himself. He valued a midfielder that understood that when the defense is struggling, he has to get into the thick of the action, and not just wait in the middle of the park for the defense to sort the problem out. He would understand that any goal scored by the opposition was a goal conceded by the team, not just the defense. Moreover, as a part of the team, that meant that if they allowed a goal to be scored, the whole team was a goal down, not just the defense.

Sounds simple, but he witnessed too many players that were unwilling to do that. Sometimes, a star player would emerge that was only in it for himself. Catterick was legendary for bypassing that player. And even though he received so much criticism from the media and every armchair fan in the country, he knew what he wanted and stuck to his plan. However, even that prima dona of a player would understand why he was not selected.

Any professional coach knows that it can be just as difficult, if not more so, to manage the expectations of the media and the fans; however, to be completely successful, a coach needs to learn this skill, as well. There were many of his peers that ignored this fact and, after falling out of grace with this group, had ultimately lost their job with a vote of no confidence. This had never happened to Bob Catterick.

As a manager, he had also won the most coveted prize in football, or soccer — the World Cup. The amazing thing about this is that he used his full squad of players, as the game required, not just the same predictable few. And he switched formations throughout the competition. Sometimes he played 4-4-2; sometimes he played three defenders with five midfielders and two strikers; and other times he would play with wing-backs (attacking full-backs) with three in midfield. It all depended on what he felt was the best way to exploit the weaknesses of the opposition. He was never looking for a playing style to merely neutralize them; his only intention was to win. And win he invariably did.

After enjoying the glory of World Cup victory, Bob felt the need to re-evaluate his life. He had reached the pinnacle of his career in sports — but what now? He considered trying his hand at another professional sport and putting his management style to the test. But that idea didn't get his juices flowing. Neither did becoming a sports analyst.

Bob had a close friend who was the CEO of a major international corporation. After several discussions, his friend invited him to leave the glamorous world of sports and move into the cutthroat world of business. His friend had convinced him that knowing the product was only a fraction of what was needed to be successful; the key was leadership, and Bob had a proven record of accomplishment in this area.

The friend (Tom Kendall) was a shrewd and successful businessman. He had steered his company from relative obscurity to the rankings of the Fortune 50. He knew what it took to make it work in the corporate world.

Bob accepted the position of Vice President of Customer Relations. His decision startled the sports world. Nobody could quite understand why he would leave the arena in which he had been so successful and begin all over again at the age of 57.

For their part, the leadership at the company he was about to join viewed his appointment with suspicion. They were sure that this was another great publicity stunt by their CEO, utilizing Bob's celebrity status — after all, his management experience was largely irrelevant to the business world. Surely, they mused, he was not actually going to take over the reins of such a crucial part of the organization. Surely, he would only be good for signing autographs. Prior to Bob's first day, Tom met with his senior management team and explained that Bob would be a director within the organization, with the same level of accountability as the rest of the team.

And so, the stage was set — Bob Catterick was to begin his new career.

During his first few months, he met with all of his staff, and began the learning process of the business he now represented. This was a very different situation for him. It was nothing like he had imagined — it was much worse. After six months, productivity was down, sales were flat, employee turnover was up, and complaints from both customers and employees were up. Bob did not know what had hit him. It was on a day that the company directors had a scheduled meeting that change was to become a constant. This was never going to be a pleasant meeting. There were many problems with which the organization was grappling, many of which emanated from Bob's departments. There was going to be a fair amount of finger-pointing and most of them would be aimed directly at him.

He wondered if this would be a good time to resign. Yet, in all the years as a soccer coach, when pressure was at its highest, he had never quit. He had convinced himself that he was not a quitter. He knew that with the right employer, who would give him enough time, things would always turn out to the liking of the fans (his customers) and directors alike.

He had learned to smile in the face of adversity. But this was different: he actually did not know what he was doing and did wonder, albeit momentarily, if Tom had made a terrible decision when he had enticed Bob to the world of business. The meeting was every bit as bad as Bob could ever have imagined.

The attendees were:

Tom Kendall – Chief Executive Officer (CEO)

Bob Catterick – V.P. Customer Relations

Phil Royal – V.P. Sales and Marketing

Daley Walker – V.P. Human Resources

Judy Harvey – CFO

Keith Smith – V.P. of Operations

After everyone has settled into their seats, Tom stood up, cleared his throat, and began his remarks. With his eyes fixed on Bob, everyone in the room knew this was going to be a public dismissal. Tom had done this before. They all remembered the time when one of their team had been so negligent that Tom had publicly accused him of ruining his company and instantly dismissed him.

However, there was some level of sympathy for Bob; after all, he was a national hero. Everyone could remember dancing around the living room as the national team scored the winning goal in the last World Cup. The players did well because of Bob's leadership and technical genius. But this was not a soccer match, this was the real world and Bob was better off going back to where he was at his best. Anyway, his country needed him!

"Bob," Tom began, "in all your years as a soccer coach, which would you say was the most difficult period?" There was a deafening silence. Almost everyone, including Bob, wondered what the point of this discussion was going to be. Emotions were running high and the CEO was becoming nostalgic. "What was he doing?" they all thought. Given the circumstances, even Bob looked uncomfortable. Tom stared attentively at his target, but stood patiently, waiting for the answer. After a couple of moments, Bob began his response: "By far, the hardest games were the early stages of the cup."

"Why was that?" asked Tom.

"For the managers, soccer is like a game of chess. Every player has a set of skills that fits nicely into the team as a whole. Each player is considered on his own merits but is useless to me if they do not consider the whole team, since each team plays slightly differently. For example, if we were playing against a team that played the long-ball style where they hoofed the ball high into the air from the back of the park up to the strikers, It would be pointless to fill my midfield with talented individuals because the ball was invariably going to be launched over their heads towards my defenders. In these games, my play had to build up from the defense. As long as we could maintain possession of the ball, our play could pass through the midfield to our front men."

"How different was the criteria for each player in a game

like that?" Tom enquired.

"I needed big and powerful defenders," Bob responded. "They had to be able to cope with the high-ball bombardment that would be constantly dumped into the penalty area and they also had to cope with the aerial competency of the opposition's strikers. I needed fit midfielders with quick minds to be able to move up and down the field of play, as the game required. These midfielders had to be stand-in defenders when necessary and wingers with an ability to cross the ball at other times. In fact, the whole dynamics of the team would be very different from when we would play a team that kept the ball on the ground."

"How so?" asked Tom.

"For these sorts of games, we needed a dominant midfield that was creative. I would play with greater numbers in the midfield because they became the team's engine. I would need creative players that could drop the ball with deadly accuracy. My strikers didn't only need to be deadly in front of goal; I needed them to create space by running off the ball for the midfielders to come through."

"That's very interesting," said Tom.

"This is all very well and good," screamed the V.P. of Sales (Phil Royal), "and in another setting I would be very interested to hear this, but this has nothing to do with what we are here for." His comments were followed by a few nods around the room as others wondered where this was going.

"Oh, I think this has everything to do with it," responded Tom. "How many of you have considered your plan before going into the game of business? I don't just mean the plan of what we have to get done — the tasks for the day. How many of you have considered if your team is balanced and if you have the right skill-mix for each battle in which you were engaged, so that your chances of creating a winning formula would be greatly enhanced? Bob called them his midfielders; I call them our creative thinkers. We would expect many of them to be in our marketing department, but are they all in there? Of course they are not, but where are they — do you know?

Did you notice how he spoke of his midfielders needing to be the team's engine? These are the people that should get this company moving again. We have been squashing them for far too long. What would happen to this company if, instead, we started encouraging them? We need them to be creative, and when the pressure is on they have to be able to change the direction or style of play, or rather our methods of operation, the products and services we supply, and with little warning — just like Bob's winning team. But first we have to identify them; then we have to change the culture of our organization and allow them to make the moves they think are best, without placing too many restrictions on their decision-making!

"Can you imagine if one of Bob's midfielders had to run to the side of the playing field and ask if it's OK to swing the ball down the left side of the field, because he had noticed that the defender on their side was having a bad day? At the very least, his indecisiveness would cost him his position in the team, and in a worst-case scenario, he would give the ball away. And yet, in this company, we require our people to ask us permission to do their job everyday."

Turning his attention to the sales and marketing Vice President, Tom said, "Phil, when you lost your best sales agent, how did you go about finding a replacement?"

Phil responded: "We placed an advertisement in the technical journal and on the applicant tracking system and asked HR to sift through the resumes as they came in."

"Yes, and as I recall, that's about all the information we could get out of you," said Daley Walker, the HR Vice President as knowing chuckles rippled around the room.

Turning the attention back to Phil, Tom asked: "What were you looking for?"

"Someone with sales experience and lots of energy. I felt losing Sandy Brown had put us at a significant competitive disadvantage. I wanted someone just the same as her. We had to try and regain as much of her experience as we could find."

"And yet," Tom interrupted, "you and I had been talking for months about how your team is very good at what we have done for years, but nobody offers anything new. We both know that if I were to demand that your department produce a new approach to the sales challenge, the best you would do is give me a variation of what we already do."

"Sounds like my defenders." interjected Bob.

"How is that?" asked Phil.

"The last thing I need as a coach of a soccer team is a creative defender. His role does not call for creativity, he just has to stop the ball getting anywhere near the goal. I need him to work in perfect harmony with the rest of the defenders so that they work as a unit. If the rest of the defense get confused over what one of their unit is going to do once they have the ball, the result would be utter confusion, which is easy for the opposition to exploit."

"Exactly," said Tom enthusiastically. "Those predictable types are important, but we can't have a whole team of them. What you should have done," turning his attention back to Phil, "is not only look for someone who had the technical skills, but also someone that could demonstrate they were capable of finding that third alternative. The one who is better than you and I are on our own!"

"She has done an outstanding job," said Phil, defensively, referring to his replacement hire.

"Indeed she has," said Tom, "but she has never contributed to the team. Everything she has done has been as an individual contributor. Thank heavens she had the back-up of a dedicated administration department."

"That has been no small task." Piped up the Vice President of Finance, Judy Harvey. "She is not one for detail. It is only due to the experience of my team members, catching inaccuracies in her paperwork that have prevented some own goals," she said, happy she could add an analogy to the theme of the discussion. As she was looking around with a huge smile on her face, waiting for the accolades from the rest of the group, Tom brought her back to the discussion: "Nice analogy, but let's take a look at your department. You have a department full of what Bob would call his defenders, the group that doesn't cause you any surprises, that knows its business and is very detailed and consistent. You also have a nice blend of people that are creative and are able to come up with customized solutions for our customers' needs, but you have nobody that finishes, other than yourself."

"That would be my strikers," chirped Bob.

"What?" asked Keith, Vice President of operations.

"The responsibility of my strikers is to get the ball in the

27

back of the opposition's net — to finish the job or see that it happens. I expect my defenders and midfielders to work together, during an attack, until they deliver the ball in, or around, the opposition's penalty area. Once delivered, my strikers are paid a lot of money to finish the job and put the ball in the only place it hurts — so we win the game. It makes very little difference how well everyone else does, if we can't score goals. They just have to be clinical and have the drive to finish the job."

"Keith," began Tom, "I think I can now see that you put very little thought into that aspect of your team."

"Well, I don't employ soccer players," he said, sarcastically.

"That's true, but I think you're missing the point. If you had applied this style of thinking when you replaced that young lady two months ago, you would have looked for someone who could give your department that killer instinct. Synergistically speaking, you would have found someone that, when all the effort was over, they would have made sure jobs were finished. Just like last week when you were on that training course. Our biggest customer let us know that we had delivered the wrong parts. It was 5 o'clock in the evening and everyone was going home. That supervisor of yours, what's her name?"

"Sarah," said Keith

"That's right, Sarah," recalled Tom. Sarah had called a meeting and a solution was found. It was decided that someone would make use of the delivery transportation was already making its way to the airport by having them take the correct parts out on the same drop; this would ensure the customer had the correct parts by the morning. That was all well and good, and although Frank did go down and speak with transportation, nobody ensured the correct parts were packaged and ready for delivery.

"Transportation thought you were delivering to them a package ready to go, but your guy just assumed transportation would do that, and all he had to do was take the parts to them.

"You can tell where this story is going, can't you?" This was one of Tom's rhetorical questions, and they all knew better than to answer it.

"Unfortunately," Tom continued, "when the truck left, the parts were still in the depot — nobody in transportation, knew what they were there for."

Almost spontaneously, Bob grabbed a pen and began drawing on the flip chart. He said, "The problem was identified and Sarah (a defender) called a meeting. A solution was found (midfield creativity) to take the correct parts to transportation. What was missing in this process was the person to finish the plan (the striker)." A normal team formation would look like this:

Team Model

4-4-2

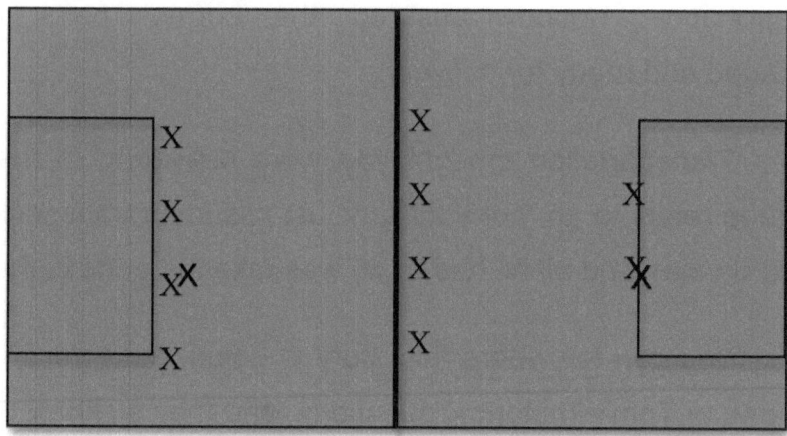

However, in this case, the team had no strikers. Not only was the team incomplete, there was nobody to finish the job even if the ball had been placed at the right end.

"I think I'm beginning to understand," said Judy. "The defenders are the consistent people. They are the ones who come into work every day, and just plain do their job. These are our reliable people who do the job the same way. The best natural defenders work well as a team when given the chance. You just know what to expect from them. When things are struggling, they are probably the ones who would pick up the slack. When the work was ready, they would deliver it to the strikers who would finish the job by delivering the deliverables. In this case, they would have noticed the package needed to be prepared for delivery, not just dumped in the transportation manager's office."

"Great summary," said Tom. "Phil, what about the midfielders?"

Phil responded: "They are the group that can motivate us with exciting new ideas and approaches. They're a tireless lot who are comfortable working outside of the box and making sure we aren't predictable to our competitors."

"Yes!" shouted Bob.

"Wait a minute," said Tom, rather pensively. "It's OK for the competition to be confused about what we might do next, and it's great to catch them off-guard with our tactics, but how does that sort of behavior affect our customers? Won't it irritate them just a little bit if they can't figure out what we stand for? Won't we find it difficult to attract new customers if they don't know who we are? And what about the benefactor in all of this, the shareholders; we certainly don't want them getting confused, do we?" The room fell silent. Tom could see that, if he was not careful, he would begin to lose the momentum that had been gathering steam. Just when he was getting ready to answer his own question, Bob spoke.

"There's something we haven't covered yet," he said pensively. "What about us in this room? As the team leaders in our respective departments, where do we play during the game? I mean, what position should we be playing in?"

Jan, showing some confidence, spoke up, "We would naturally play wherever we are best suited."

"But isn't it our job to be the final defender of the company values and standards?" asked Bob. "Isn't it up to us to be the champion of team and group activities? I'm not sure we can do that if we are so involved in constantly running around the field of play — the shop floor. And surely, it is our job to ensure that those creative people — our midfielders, are under control and not performing like loose cannons under the company banner. You know, wasting time searching for the sexy answer, ignoring the obvious solution."

"Bob, what are you getting at?" asked Tom with a smile.

"Well we can't very well be strikers, because for much of the game, we would be playing with our back to the rest of the team. If our natural style puts us in midfield, who is going to ground us while we are busy trying to come up with all of these new approaches? And if we are in the role of defender, what happens if the opposition gets beyond us? It seems that none of these positions would be suitable for the team leader."

"So where should we be playing?" Asked Tom.

The goalkeeper!" said Keith, as if a light had suddenly switched on.

"So you're saying that, as managers of our own teams, we belong in the role as the goalkeeper?" asked Phil.

"I think I am." Bob Said. "That would make us the final defender of company values. If the rest of the team's efforts are failing, it becomes the job of the goalkeeper to be the final defender. In the same way in business, I suppose, the goal-keeper is the one person that can observe for much of the game, and if the team does make mistakes and the opposition is through on goal, ready to pounce on our vulnerable market share, then the final defender is called into action. On his own, he is very vulnerable, and outfield players (our team members) have been known to score own goals sometimes, too, or make costly mistakes. It is at times like this that the goalkeeper, us, is all that is between our own goal (market share) and a daunting striker from the other team, or competition."

There was a moment of silence. It was almost a reverent feeling that came over the room, as each leader had a quiet moment of reflection on the world that had just been opened to them.

At this point, Tom thought the team had done enough. Without anyone really noticing, the business has closed down for the day and everyone else had gone home. He decided to let this team of executives retire for the day and sleep on the ideas that had been discussed and suggested a meeting in a week's time. Everyone cleared their schedules and committed to the agreed time. During the days that followed that first meeting, each of the team began looking at their people through a new set of eyes. They began to see who were the defenders, and who were their creative people (the midfielders) and who were the people that had that special ability of seeing quickly and accurately and then ensuring a high success rate in delivery (the predator). But one question remained and that would have to be addressed at the next meeting.

Finally, the day arrived for them to meet again.

After the initial greetings, Tom got right down to business. "OK, we have had a week to think about our business and take a look at each of our teams. I hope you noticed that this company is made up of several teams." Turning to the dry-wipe board, Tom wrote each of the teams:

- The company.

- Each of your own departments.

- This team — the senior management group sitting here in this room.

They all nodded. Then Bob asked the question that was on everyone's mind, "I understand the concept of all of this — I should, I've lived and breathed it all my life." Everyone smiled - now Bob was one of them, and it sort of felt that he belonged, after all. "But what I don't understand is how do we actually know how to place each member of our team in their positions?"

"I was thinking the same thing," said Keith. "There has to be some way of us all using the same criteria; otherwise we will not have a consistent approach to this, and that could negatively impact the cohesion," he said, pointing to Tom's list on the board.

"I've been thinking about this, too," said Daley. "And I think I have a solution."

As everyone turned to look at the Vice President of Human Resources, Tom asked him to take the floor and tell everyone about the work that he had done to support the team concept.

This was Daley's opportunity to contribute in a major way. He began, "Using the Meyer's-Briggs personality types I have been able to place everyone in the team in the positions Bob introduced to us."

"So what is Meyer's-Briggs?" asked Bob.

"Good question," said Daley. "There are lots of psychometric tests out there. I looked at many of them and determined that, for our purposes, this one is the most suitable. Meyer's-Briggs is a way of understanding individuals on a very personal level. By using this assessment we can better understand each person who works here. After we have completed this part we will have a consistent measurement for our teams."

"So how does it work?" Asked Keith.

Daley handed out a piece of paper with each of the sixteen personality types listed:

ESTJ   PRAGMATIC

ISTJ   GUARDIAN

INFP   ADVOCATE

INFJ   PERFECTIONIST

ENTJ   CHAIRPERSON

ESFJ   HARMONIOUS

ISFP   TRADITIONALIST

ISFJ   ANCHOR

ENFP	THE INTUITIVE
ENTP	IDEA TALISMAN
INTP	IDEA GENERATOR
INTJ	EXTREME CONCEPTUALIZER
ENFJ	POPULAR COMMUNICATOR
ESTP	ACTION-TRIGGERED
ESFP	THE OPTIMIST
ISTP	IMPULSE BUYER

As each of the team looked over the list, Daley continued, "I think it is appropriate for us now to find out how this team fits together."

Team Model

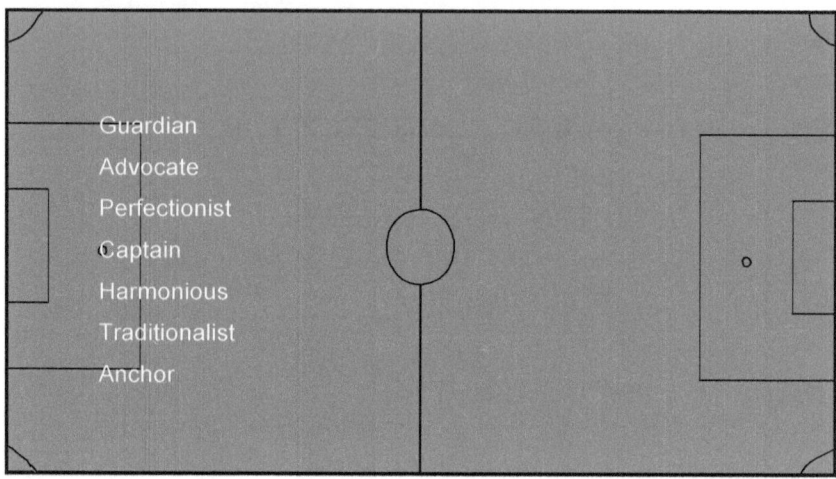

She then guided them through the process of the test and collected the results, and announced to the group, "before we identify where each of us fits on the field of play, let's take a closer look at the list I gave you and which personality type fits where. Daley then placed a large copy of a soccer field on the wall and began placing the defenders in place first:

"There may be some crossover, such as in the case of the INTP, but let's go through each one and understand why each one fits into the defense." Daley then went through each personality type.

ISTJ: The Guardian: This is the quintessential thinker. There can never be enough detail for this person. They are practical in nature, dependable, and persistent. This person is a steady rock in the heart of the defense. They are not going to give you any surprises and will defend the rules with every ounce or energy they possess.

ISFJ: The Anchor: This person does not understand when to go home. They are workhorses that just stay at the job until it is done. They are at home in a traditional environment and are resistant to change. If a procedure is established, the ISFJ is not going to challenge it. Routines are not boring to this type of person; they can get on with the same task, or tasks, and be consistently enthusiastic about them.

ESTJ: The Pragmatist: If this person is ever working in an environment where there is little structure, this is the person who will place disciplines and processes. They love details, and are the most loyal and dutiful in the defensive makeup of the team. Probably the best way to describe this player is 'steady.' Again, like the ISFJ, they are great in a routine task and will not get distracted.

ENTJ: The Captain: As I mentioned before, this person capable of coming up with new ways to play the game. They are very much take-charge people, and can be relied upon to mobilize the troops and ensure everyone has a job to do. The stereotypical ENTJ loves change, but only if they are the catalyst of the change; otherwise they can be quite resistant to it and some may see them as a blocker, therefore placing them squarely in the defense. However, that could lead to job dissatisfaction if they are held in routine tasks.

ISFP: The Traditional Artist: This is the person you can be sure will care about the people aspect of tasks to be done. This is also the flower child that believes things are best left well alone. They may understand that change is necessary, but they would never be the ones to find new ways or methods. For this type, life can be a beautiful journey that does not need to be bettered; people just need to get on with it.

INFP: The Advocate: I found this person type difficult to place. I think they could be a predator but for the fact that they tend to spend an inordinate amount of time on introspection. They are a searcher, not of ideas, but of a better self. Although they tend to be idealistic in nature, they are clearly defenders of the values that are in place, and are fiercely committed to a cause, and strangely, like the ISFP, avoid constant conflict. For these reasons, I have placed them in the defense. They also have abilities that would make them good in a goal-scoring role."

INFJ: The Perfectionist: The INFJ is a great team player — always there to offer help and support to other team members. The "N" in this equation does lean them towards a natural creative side to their nature, but this group is also meticulous. No detail escapes them. This can make them invaluable in the planning stages. This group can be used to analyze data in great depth, to ensure that we have not made any mistakes with whatever the task is at hand.

ESFJ: The Harmonious: This group is a very traditional group of people. In their effort to support what already is — the status quo — they can also be relied upon to try to reach a consensus with everyone else. Harmony is important to them and you can be sure they will try to reach it, because disharmony is something they just cannot abide. They will stick to the task, networking until they get it. Watch out, though, they can be a little emotional in the process."

Daley paused. There was a buzz in the room and energy levels were high.

Tom suggested a break for the day and a return the next day, saying with a smile, "We still have a business to run. Tomorrow we can take a look at another section of the team." Reluctantly everyone left the room.

It was a strange feeling that prevailed that day. Usually, when a meeting had concluded, no matter how important the agenda was, the focus quickly turned to the tasks at hand, as each of the senior management team went their separate ways. That was no different on this day, except they were going back wondering who were the best people to get those tasks done, and seemed to have a different perspective on why certain tasks had not been completed as well as they would have liked.

There were no great calamities that occurred in the business during their last session, so when the time came for the next one, they were just as eager to get started.

Once assembled, Keith (in his usual impatient manner) said, "I think we should spend some time identifying where we each fit on the team."

Tom said, "What do the rest of you think about that?"

"I agree," said Bob, with Phil nodding in agreement.

"I don't think that is the best use of our time," said Judy. "I think we should complete the decision make-up of the team, move to the creative people and then finish with us."

Tom and Daley glanced at each other and both smiled. Tom responded, "I think this is the right thing to do. What do you think, Daley?"

Daley responded: "I agree. I think once we have finished the team balance sheet, we will not need to do much work on which of us fits where. I think it will become pretty obvious."

"Then let's get going," said Phil. Daley again took the floor, replacing the field of play on the wall, this time showing the goal scorers. "Today, we are going to do just as Judy suggested.

Team Model

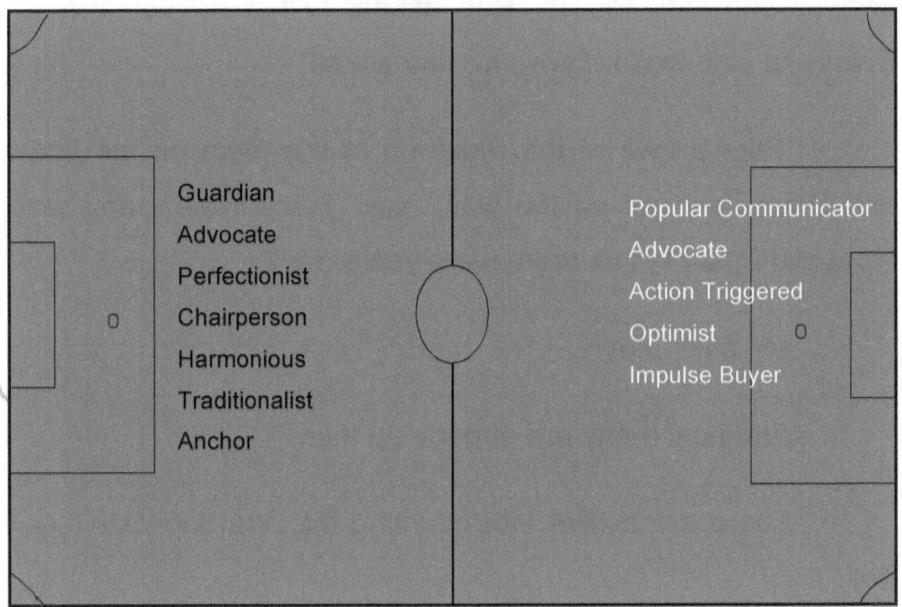

We are going to finish the parts of the team involved in the decision-making — the operators, the finishers. We are going to look at the goal scorers. Remember that these are the people that respond to the adulation of the kill. These are the people that will work alone, if necessary, but will take a good plan and execute it, sniffing a goal-scoring opportunity where others would still want to take time to talk about it.

"Does anyone notice anything interesting about how the team is looking on that board?" asked Tom.

The room was silent. It always went like that when nobody really understood the question. Rather than take a stab at the answer and look foolish, Bob asked, "What do you mean?" Everyone else was relieved he had asked.

"Take a look at the make-up of the team on the board that Daley has put on the wall," said Tom. "How many team types did Daley tell us there were yesterday?"

"16" said Judy.

"And how many are already up there?"

"There are twelve, not counting the one duplicate," said Phil.

"Actually, that is interesting," added Judy. "Unless there is a lot of duplicating for the midfielders, this would suggest that there are fewer people to choose from who are comfortable truly thinking outside the box. It means we may have to search a little more to find those people to evenly balance our teams. There are the people that are better at finishing the job, people that are the defenders, who are our reliable action people and are consistent day-in-day-out. And then the people that are the midfielders — the creative force in the business. We just have to be diligent in finding the right blend of talent."

"I hadn't thought of it in quite that way before," said Daley.

"If the majority of people are not excited about possibilities, it means we have to be pretty focused during our interviewing stages because we could end up with a bunch of people that don't have the staying power to get a job done. I suppose we could end up with a department that only excels in analyzing existing data and delivering what we already do, but could be short on new ideas," added Tom.

"Perhaps that is one reason why we are spending so much money on sub-contracting work out, because the workforce we currently have is at its best after all the wrinkles have already been ironed out," said Judy.

"Good point!" It seemed that Keith was finally beginning to understand. It was because tasks were taking too long to finish, that Keith had taken the step, a few years ago, to out-source much of the detail work. "This is good stuff. The application of this are pretty broad." He continued, "I could save money by either developing the skills in the people I have, or by being more careful in selecting the right people for hire."

"I guess this is the same thing we were talking about a few weeks ago when we first started all of this," said Phil, "when Tom brought up the sales person I hired to fill the vacancy."

"Yep, the same principle," said Tom.

"You must remember," said Daley, "that those with an N in the configuration of letters definitely have a creative side, but they are not always innovative. They may be excellent conceptual thinkers, that is, they can design some wonderful alternatives to existing ideas, but not necessarily innovative ideas. The truly creative minds could take a blank piece of paper and create something quite extraordinary."

Since there was no comment on that, Daley continued. "Let's take a closer look at the goal scorers," said Daley, taking back control of the group.

"Why don't we refer to them as our predators?" suggested Bob. "These are people that can sniff out a goal-scoring opportunity."

"OK," said Daley. "Let's take a look at these predators in more detail."

ENFJ: The Popular Communicator: The ENFJ is likely to shoot from the hip and is usually pretty accurate. If they rely on their intuition, they can usually size up a situation pretty quickly. They are not detailed and tend to get a little restless if they are required to get involved in too much of it. Planning is not really their thing. Interestingly, they often have an expectation that others will just follow their lead; it doesn't always happen, and when it doesn't, they are surprised. Because of their quick decision-making, I have placed them as a predator.

INFP: The Advocate: As I mentioned yesterday, the INFP is comfortable both in defense, and in a goal-scoring opportunity. A predator has to enjoy a certain amount of stand- alone time. This type is comfortable in their own company and work well on their own. Although they are patient with complicated situations (skills of a defender) routine details have no interest to them. This type also struggles with the abstract, and prefers something to be ready for them before they get involved.

ESTP: Action-Triggered: People of this personality are action-oriented. They are excited by the action of action. They can be a little flamboyant and are deadly accurate in assessing the competition and those around them. They are good at seizing a moment of opportunity and are ideal predators. This person would get tired of mundane roles and detail, but enjoy the thrill of the here-and-now.

ESFP: The Optimist: This impulsive character is usually the life and soul of any party. Life is never dull for them. They are at their best in active jobs; therefore, if you need someone to sift through details of a project, this is not the person to consider for the job. They can be swayed by the opinions of others and are at their best when things are going well. This is not the sort of person you would want during the planning stages of any project, but would jump at the opportunity to make it work with deadly accuracy.

ISTP: The impulse Buyer: This loner tends to be impulsive. They communicate through what they do, rather than through planning. This type is deadly accurate and is fearless regardless of the risk to themselves. They are attracted to excitement like bees to honey and are turned on when the odds are stacked against them. If the ISTP is focused on scoring the goal, they will do it, and anyone who gets in their way would wish they hadn't. They can be perfectly happy waiting for that opportunity to leap into action and so would be comfortable in long periods of lull, but would typically be ready to pounce the moment opportunity arrives. This is the ultimate predator."

Once again, Tom stepped in and ended the meeting. During his closing remarks, he went over some key operational issues that were discussed around the table briefly. The meeting was adjourned until tomorrow.

This was to be the final day of introduction to the Meyer's- Briggs theory of character and temperament types. As usual, Tom opened the meeting and explained what would happen in this meeting. There would be no discussion, at this point, on the senior team, other than a disclosure of who was which type, and that this was to be a catalyst in changing the culture of the organization. Tom then handed the remainder of the time over to Daley.

Once again, placing the field of play on the wall, Daley recapped the last two days of discussion, and then proceeded.

"We are going to finish our discussion by talking about the smallest group of people. Again using the book Please Understand Me, by David Keirsey and Marilyn Bates, we now find that, not only are there fewer personality types that can comfortably operate in the midfield, but, within those types they are a smaller percentage of the world's population. So let's take a closer look:

Team Model

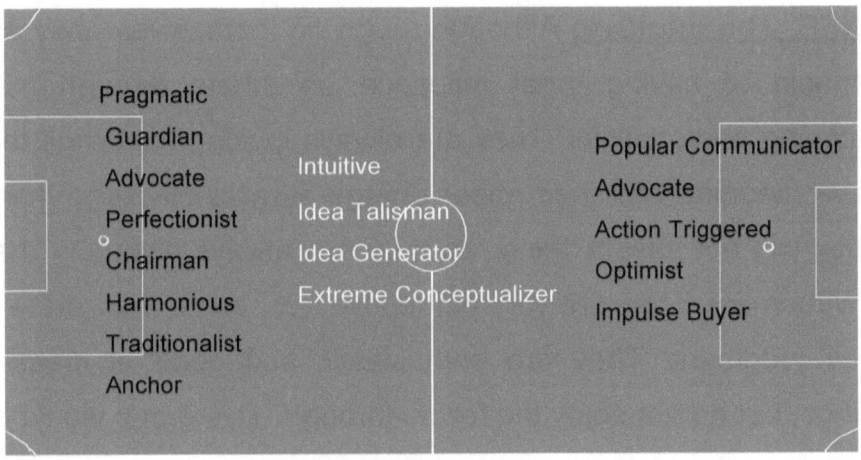

Pragmatic
Guardian
Advocate
Perfectionist
Chairman
Harmonious
Traditionalist
Anchor

Intuitive
Idea Talisman
Idea Generator
Extreme Conceptualizer

Popular Communicator
Advocate
Action Triggered
Optimist
Impulse Buyer

Bob commented, "The midfield group is interesting. Two E's and two I's."

Doing some further analysis, Keith offered, "Out of the four, three are NP's, and all four are N's."

"That's right," said Daley. "If you remember, I said earlier that those with an N in their character type lean more to the creative side, and so that means those who have an S in their type lean more towards the practical, 'don't rock the boat' side."

"So you would expect the midfield to only have N's there, rather than S's," said Phil.

"That's correct, Phil. Good observation, Keith," said Tom.

Daley continued: "Let's finish today by taking a look at those midfielders in closer detail.

ENFP: The Intuitive: Although tough on themselves, they are capable of having great influence on others through their outgoing personalities. They are always looking for things that have meaning and their sheer energy attracts others to them. They will not miss a thing, as they are always scanning their environment. They are very perceptive but can be inaccurate in their judgment. They are enthusiastic and good at creating things, but do not enjoy the follow-through. This group would be particularly useful in trying to find new techniques, processes, systems, methods and in making recommendations, but not so good if we asked them to test their theories; routine is certain to bore the ENFP.

ENTP: The Idea Talisman: Any team is lucky to have such an entrepreneur in their midst. This type is alert to possibilities and will balk against suggestions that things are done just because that is the way we have always done them. This outgoing type is ready to challenge everything and make recommendations for improvement. They balance this with a love of the complex, and so would be able to come up with a complete plan rather than just an idea for development. If there were levels of performance within this small group of midfielders, then this would be the part of the team that did the quality inspection before releasing it to the defenders to critique.

INTJ: The Extreme Conceptualizer: This type is a tenacious builder of systems. Always looking to the future, and insistent that ideas or practices have some use, they are the least likely to be impressed with titles or authority. They are just as likely to challenge the president of the company, as they are the janitors on their first day, the good thing is that they are no respecter of persons and would be unlikely to provide an opportunity to any authority that might abuse their position. As long as an idea makes sense, this creative machine-like person will adopt any idea. They will drive an idea until it no longer serves a purpose and then go in search of another idea. If they find one that belongs to someone else, they are happy to dismantle it and re-design it to fit their purposes. They are equally capable of finding something so far out of the ordinary that others may find themselves feeling inadequate around them. Combine them with the perception others have that the INTJ can see right through them; you have a very commanding figure that is strong enough to withstand any criticism that may come.

INTP: The Idea Generator: this type has a tremendous capacity for concentration; able to detect error in almost anything, they are capable of identifying what may be wrong instantly. This capability would also make them effective predators, except they are not grounded in reality, it is ideas that get them excited, and it is after generating the ideas they are happy to turn it over to the likes of an INTJ or ENTP for further work and study before passing the idea, or project, over to the defenders for their input."

In conclusion, Tom spoke: "I want you each to know that I am committed to this process for identifying existing and future talent. We must now go through the exercise and identify where we are short on the talent we need; whether it be in defense, the people that analyze; in midfield, the people that give us solutions; or the predators, the people that make it happen. None of this work will change unless we are all committed to it, and it occurs to me that you will only make it happen when yagottawanna. The opposite of this is yadontgottawanna, and it is obvious to me that your team and my team won't win if ya don't."

SECOND HALF

GAME PLAN ONE

THE VISION

Managing a business group is not that different from managing a sports team. In fact, there is a strong similarity between successful teams in both arenas. In this book, I have chosen to compare them to the game of soccer, but the concept could work just as well in any team sport.

The people you work with are the players on your team; playing on a soccer field are players. Your people are employed by the company to make the organization successful (win the game). Each person is employed to fulfill a specific role, and sometimes the organization will have to change its style to make a system of approach work for the players they currently have at their disposal. It could be a costly mistake to force people to play, or work, out of position — that's when things go wrong.

A soccer team is divided into three areas, defense, midfield, and attack. A good team has experts playing in each of these areas on the field of play. Those who work best in defense form a slick unit that works well together. This group is not comfortable with surprises, never taking unnecessary risks; the midfielders are the playmakers and have the ability to mix up the play at anytime; the strikers, or as I have referred to them earlier — predators — have the task of finishing the job, thereby placing pressure on the opposition by scoring goals at every opportunity, in predatory fashion. Together, all parts of the team form a synergy, and, like clockwork, operate clinically to overpower the opposition and win the game.

In the same way, a successful work team has to have defined areas of expertise. And when I say this, I'm not referring to one department such as marketing, as compared to another department such as HR. The team has to have people that are consistent, that are creative, that are instinctive and can smell weakness in the opposition and exploit it, thereby winning the "game" for the company. In this book, I have broken down the make-up of a successful work-team into the same three areas as in a soccer team, and to do this I have used the personality profiling of Meyer's-Briggs. In the absence of a more closely aligned psychometric test, Meyer's-Briggs works well. After completing the testing, each of the sixteen possibilities fits into at least one of the three areas on the field of play. For example, SJ's (as in ESTJ, ISTJ, ESFJ, ISFJ from the Meyer's-Briggs assessment tool) fit nicely into the defense, whereas midfielders and predators have their own unique combinations.

Not all of the roles are easily inter-changeable. If a natural defender is asked to be a striker too often, the result is likely to be burnout, because the skill set, or mindset, of a defender is different: one is like a marathon runner (the defender) and the other is a sprinter (predator). Imagine asking a 26-mile marathon runner to compete in a 100-meter sprint race! Perhaps the athlete would hold his, or her, own for the first race, but the likelihood is that they would completely mis-time their race, and would not be prepared for the burst of energy each of this runner's competitors come prepared to demonstrate. The principle is similar for a sprinter asked to run a marathon, they may be tempted to exert too much energy too early, getting tired long before the finishing line is in sight, and, if that happens, the race, for them, is over. The sprinter is turned on by the thrill of speed and an immediate end in sight, just like a predator, who has to see a goal in front of him or her to get excited. The marathon runner is more strategic and happy to play a patient waiting game, similar to the defender. The roles are very different.

The people who fit comfortably into the role of midfield would find the role of defender too tedious in the long term, and would likely lose interest, whereas they may find the role of the predator to be too intense. Although midfielders don't mind getting their hands dirty as they get involved in some sort of cause, they don't tend to have the killer instinct of the striker. And so it is, if you were a top coach of a top team, you would not expect one of your star strikers to play just as well in a defensive role. Some can, but most just get in the way. It's fair to say that many skilled defenders complain that strikers are awkward in the back and have a poor concept of how to feed the ball forward rather than shoot it forward.

Placing a naturally left-footed player on the other side of

the park can cause another problem, and although this can be a good tactical move, doing it accidentally could spell disaster. And what kind of soccer manager wouldn't know which foot is the preferred one for each of the players? And yet many business managers make these kinds of mistakes too often. Make mistakes if you must, but make them on purpose.

Knowing your own team is important, but you will make naïve decisions about each game played, if you fail to understand the team you are competing against. You must understand what they are good at, and fully understand their weaknesses and strengths so you can exploit them and prevent them from playing to their strengths. In the next chapter, we will look at what is important to know about those who would love to steal your place in the market, and eventually see your team relegated to the recreational leagues of the business in which you compete.

GAME PLAN TWO

THE OPPOSITION

Like any soccer coach, as with a business manager, each game you play will require you to consider which players are the ones to use on a game-by-game basis. You will have to think about not only what players the opposition is likely to be using, but also what that team's preferred formation would be. For example, if you were a coach, how would you organize your team if the opposition played a very defensive style? Would it be the same formation as when you are playing a team that packs its midfield or throws in three strikers? Probably not. Your style would change to counter the style of that day's opponents. After you have decided what formation you want to play, you have to look at your team and determine which players can play at their best in the positions you have put them in on the field of play.

For example, if you acquire someone who was always a midfielder, does that automatically mean that is his, or her, best position? Let's put it another way. If you recruit someone who has always been in payroll, does that mean it is his or her best job? Perhaps that person has never been given the opportunity or any consideration for something else. And if that has been the best position for them for many years, ask yourself why that would be? It may be because they are detail-minded, or that they are very comfortable with numbers. But what if you analyzed this a little further? What if this employee had a superb customer-service attitude, coupled with a strong sense of the importance of getting people's pay correct as a part of the process that produces happy employees? Could this mean the employee who has been in payroll for many years and considered a defender for so long, is actually more suited to the role of being a predator in a customer-service role? By using this method, a manager will examine the preferred style rather than merely the experience this employee brings to the table.

Provided you have the right blend of skills to fill all of the positions you have created, and that each of those players are natural to those roles or capable of learning in another role, you now have a group of individuals ready to play at their best.

But what if you do not have the right blend of talent required for the style of game you wish to play? Playing people in unfamiliar roles is a risky business. You still have to adapt a style of play that will counter the opposition and allow your players to perform at their best, but none of this is possible if you do not know your players! You must know in what position each of your players is most comfortable playing. You have to know which positions you are unable to fill and, depending on whether you have the finances available, can then either buy the talent or develop it from within the squad to ensure a team that is competitive in every game.

Now how does this apply in the workplace? Suppose you work for a company that is a comfortable number one in its field, number one in market share, number one in profit, etc.? In these cases, the team with which you surround yourself can be very different from the team you would need if your company were struggling to survive. If your aim is to widen the gap between you and your competition, you need innovators, change drivers, and people that can catch the vision, make things happen, and drive the future to the present. This, again, is a very different set of players than those needed if your plan were to steady your business in a tough market. In this case, you would need a group of people that is reliable and tenacious – that just keeps going, no matter what. In making the impact you must make for market dominance, these are important considerations:

Know your opposition. Know where they are strong and vulnerable.

Know your own players. Know their limits and their versatility. Know where your team is in need of strengthening.

Don't be afraid to make changes to suit the current need. A star player is of no use to you if he doesn't have the team's interests at heart. You will win many more battles with a group of mediocre players, forged into a team, than you will with a squad of star players, each with their own agendas.

Changing your team doesn't necessarily mean getting rid of people: the more people you have who can fit into the first team, the more flexible your team becomes. This also does not mean you should have a huge payroll, multi-skilling or developing multi-providers (people who work well in the background, like those in administration for example, is a far cheaper way to go.)

Finally, you should consider not only the market leaders in your industry, but also the poor performers. It is a foolish tactic to ignore any other team that also plays in your industry just because you do not consider them to be good enough. Even they can change their leadership and then sneak up from behind and surprise you. Get to know why the best performers are the best; understand where they are strong, what they do well, why their customers like them so much, but don't compete with them where they are strong. Instead, spend as much time on where they are weak and build your strengths in those areas. If you are the market leader, be sure to consider those snapping at your heels, and strengthen what you already do well – those things that got you out in front – but also strengthen yourself in those areas where the competition is weak.

We have now considered the opposition and spoken briefly about your own team. In the next chapter we will spend time on what really makes your team a formidable opponent.

GAME PLAN THREE

THE MODEL

Team Model

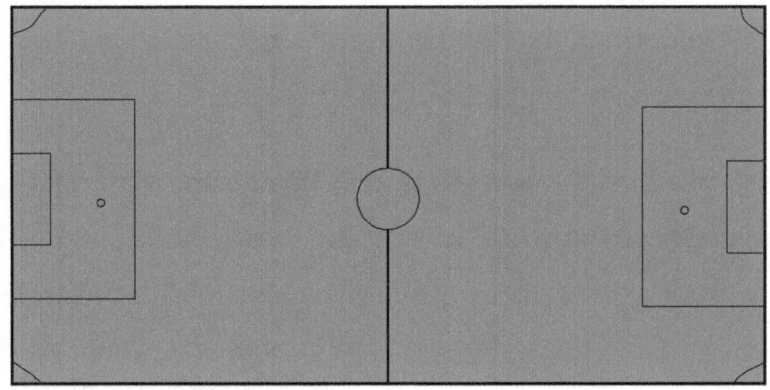

Imagine a soccer playing field — goals at each end, with penalty areas clearly marked, and a halfway line. In this chapter, we will put your team on the field of play. Any successful team has a solid defense, a creative midfield, and a potent strike force. This is not to suggest that any one group of players in a particular area of the field "owns" creativity. Everyone is creative to varying degrees; however, some are clearly more creative than others. In the words of George Orwell, "All animals are equal, but some are more equal than others" (Animal Farm). The formation of the team may remain the same for every game; however, it might change to suit the specific game being played, or have a very different look to counter the style of the opposition of the day.

Business is no different. Knowing how the opposition is likely to behave when faced with you as their competitor is a crucial factor in deciding what formation you will need to have on the field of play, and who should be in those positions. It is also vitally important, for recruitment purposes, to understand the strengths and weaknesses of your own team.

Filling a position with a person having the right skill-set for a particular role is a great relief for the hiring manager, as the talent pool seems to be getting smaller and smaller. But why would you recruit someone who cannot add value to the needs of the group as a team? Many managers recruit without really knowing what the team needs, merely what the applicant needs to do that particular job. How suicidal is that? For example, let's suppose hiring manager A has a vacancy in a children's department for a manager. The role may call for some of the following essentials:

Someone with the ability to lead

- Experience in fashion, particularly with an emphasis on children's fashion

- Experience in managing a budget

- Stock-control experience

- Employee-development skills

- Scheduling at least X number of employees

- Managing a team in retail

- Merchandising

- Marketing

And the list could go on. Everything on this list could identify a manager who may do well in their day-to-day duties; however, none of these things will identify them as an asset to the other team to which they will belong — their fellow department managers who are already running the other departments — the group of people that will collectively make decisions that grow the business. This is the other part of their role, and synergy here is necessary for the organization to flourish. It's funny how many managers seem to leave it to chance that their team will find synergy someday, somehow. Think about the group you already have employed, or that makes up the team you manage. Consider if you have a creative group, who's going to anchor them? If your group is good at executing current procedures, who comes up with new ideas? Is it the same group? Unlikely. If the business is increasing its overheads disproportionately to sales, who can

be relied upon to change the modus operandi? I bet it's you —
the boss. And if it's not you, then chances are it's not
happening, and you had better be dusting off your résumé.

Knowing the team's limitations will help you, the manager,
understand how to improve the performance of the business. If
you don't know the players in your team, you are going to
deliver a performance that is way below par — every time — or
be just plain lucky! If this is how you operate, you are playing
Russian roulette with your livelihood, and with the livelihood of
every other employee on the payroll.

The formation of the team will depend on the players you
have available. Next, we will look at the players individually;
and, for our purposes, we will start with a traditional 4-4-2
formation, that is, four defenders, four midfielders, and two
attackers.

Let's look at each section of the team in detail. (Keep in
mind that the soccer team concept is a metaphor for your work
team)

Goalkeeper

The goalkeeper is the manager of the team, the person
with whom the buck stops. Why would the manager have to go
in goal? This is because the manager is the final defender of
company values, targets, and results (see chapter six). The

person in goal should have more time to observe the action (unless the rest of the team is ineffective), and therefore, have more time to consider how the team is performing.

In the real game of team sports, the manager or coach is usually on the sidelines calling the plays; they are not prepared to get onto the field of play during a game. They often take the view that, on the day of the game, they have already done their job of coaching, assessing, etc. Besides, very few teams can claim great success with a manager who is also playing as an outfield player, so now it is up to the team to deliver. However, to ensure a winning combination in the world of business, the manager must be prepared to step into any situation. As the goalkeeper, they may be called upon to make the occasional spectacular save (and are willing to do it because they are part of the playing staff). However, they are better placed to make decisions as to whether it is time to be more creative, or to be more aggressive, or merely hold ground if they are where they can observe what's going on more than they are called into action. The difference between working ON the business rather than working IN the business.

Defenders

A good defender is someone who reads the game well and works well in a group. Defenders are reliable and are the people that you need in front of the goalkeeper to protect the goal from exposure. In a business sense, these are the plodders. They are consistent. You always know what to expect from them. These are the people who will come to work, no matter how inconvenient it may be, but they will never surprise you. The people in this group have figured out how to do their job, they have settled on what works well for them and what doesn't, and they just keep going. This does not mean they cannot be creative — they certainly can be — but their creativity is more likely to be safe, rather than an adventure. A defender is someone you would turn to when you have a task that needs doing that may take time and stamina. You would not ask this group for quick solutions, because they are perfectionists who take their time to get it right. This is the group that George Orwell would have had as his horses in Animal Farm because they are the workers. Winston Churchill must have had this group in mind when he said, in his famous speech, "We will never give up!" It seems that, no matter what you give them, they always manage to pull through, and their capacity for handling stress and a large workload is impressive. Some of them may be good conceptual thinkers (builders of existing concepts) but they are not known for their innovation (creators of fresh ideas); in fact, the notion of thinking outside the box is scary to them. Visions, which focus on the untried or unknown, will tend to make them a little twitchy. But just like everyone else on your team, defenders have weaknesses, too. They are very resistant to change. They prefer tried-and-trusted methods. They can often be heard to say: "If it ain't broke, don't fix it."

Their paradigms are typically formed from their first trainer, and may take some convincing to get them to change tactics.

They can be a bit wordy when they are trying to explain things. These are the managers who may get so bogged down in the details that people can get lost trying to remember what the objective was. They are sometimes the "naysayers," sounding a little pessimistic at times, particularly if change is being forced on them. They are the hardest group to get to buy into change. But because of their dependability, you wouldn't be without them — you couldn't be without them.

Midfielders

This is the fun group. In the game of soccer, football, or any team sport, these are the people who can effortlessly change the direction in which the game is flowing. They are not just creative thinkers; they have the confidence to try something new. They are your key players when the game needs to be shaken up a bit, when things have gone a little stale, or when the team has become a little too predictable. The last thing any successful team needs is for the opposition to be able to second-guess you. There are some professions, such as marketing, where original concepts are called for most of the time; in such an arena, this group may reign supreme, particularly when something is asked for that has never been done before.

In business terms, you would look for your midfield to provide you something you haven't had. Reducing or controlling labor turnover, or other overheads, are challenges for any organization; getting the right balance between great productivity and burning out the workforce is critical. What if you want ideas for improving communication, or offering a set of benefits that will attract the kind of employees your competition will drool over? In circumstances like these, the midfielder is the person you need to have in your team.

So what about the weaknesses of this group? One thing, for sure, is that they will need managing. Left alone for too long, they can become loose cannons. This means they could be off, doing their own thing, not necessarily what the team really needs, in search of what they find exciting. They will often miss the obvious solutions because they are attracted to the idea that nobody else has thought of. They may lack stamina and become distracted by the next exciting venture. On the other hand, they may be so full of youthful energy that they behave like Forrest Gump — running and running. When they really ought to slow down and check to make sure they aren't leaving too many people behind, confused and perhaps waning in enthusiasm because they have long forgotten what they once understood and what they were supposed to do. Every now and then you will need to tug on the reins of the midfielder, reminding them of the team objectives and bring them back in line. You must be careful, though: egos can be shallow here. In extreme cases, this group is the most likely to scare the rest of the team with their unpredictability; however, trained well, they can come up with the goods because they are unafraid of taking risks.

Predators

I could have used the term "striker" here, but I chose not to because it's interesting that the word striker sometimes refers to one who opposes change, or complains about it (as in a Union environment). It also refers to one who likes to get all the glory because their efforts have ultimately won the game. That double meaning prompted me to rename the position to "predator." A predator has the ability to sniff out opportunities with targeted accuracy. Having someone who can make things happen out of nowhere is obviously valuable to any team.

The predator is the group you want on your team because they possess that killer instinct. They can instinctively sniff out weakness in the opposition and drive the ball (or message) home from any number of difficult angles — sometimes in the face of formidable opposition (and in business, that opposition could come from outside as well as inside the company). They are predatory by nature, in the truest sense of the word. These are the people who can see an opportunity at a glance — they have great peripheral vision. They have the ability to size up the strengths and weaknesses of a plan quickly and be relied upon to make quick decisions. All predators have this instinct. The good ones are invariably accurate in their snap decisions; the ones who are not so good will still make decisions quickly, but will not base it on anything other than their "gut" feel.

This can be risky. Can you imagine being the captain of a large warship sent to destroy a target? If the ship was to have two gunners, one fires simply because the gun was loaded, and the other fires just because his sights are set. Which gunner would you choose to sail with you? In the same way, having a predator that is likely to shoot at the goal just because they have the ball, can make them a liability. It takes vision, instinct, and a willingness to work hard in a variety of different circumstances for a predator to be good. But when they are trained, they are lethal. They will win the game, sometimes single-handedly if they have to.

The thing to be mindful of is that a predator, of all of the team players, is the most likely to be a loner in the team. I'm not suggesting that this group is lonely, rather that, because of their passion to get things done, they are willing to do it completely on their own, if necessary. An individual contributor, if you will. You have to see the predator as an individual who will lose interest quickly in minutiae if it is at a planning stage. If things get too detailed, they will lose interest, and you can literally see their eyes begin to glaze over while they wait for the ball to be passed to them. It might not occur to some of them to come back and defend if the team was struggling; they would rather stand where they are most comfortable, at the other end, and cheer teammates on until the ball is somehow hoofed to them out of the defense to finish the job. You may not want them to help defend, because when they do, they have little patience with the defensive tactics, preferring instead to just hoof the ball out of the area rather than wait for the build-up. Just hoofing the ball out of the way is great if you have someone waiting to gather it, otherwise all you have done is give the ball away and found yourself on the defensive again.

In a work sense, you would not want to assign a task to this group that requires a lot of detail still to be worked through. These are the people to approach when you have a plan ready to deliver, or an idea ready to go. They are not interested in how the concept was thought up, or even the challenges that were faced as it was conceptualized. This group learns by doing. The good ones have experience and rely on a gut feeling born out of experience (or action). They get a tremendous buzz out of getting on with the job, rather than planning it. Have you ever tried to play a new game with people who just get so impatient as you struggle to understand the game's rules? These are the people who would say something like, "Can we just get on with the game? We'll worry about that if it comes up." If you have, you will understand the world of the predator — decisive, quick, and accurate, with a killer instinct but little patience for the details.

The next couple of pages will identify some suggested formations that your team should consider for different organizational needs. Following these, we will move on to consider how to select a suitable formation, or in other words, what style of behaviors you need for differing situations in the workplace.

GAME PLAN FOUR

SUITABLE FORMATIONS

Team models vary depending on what the team needs to accomplish. A few examples are as follows:

3-5-2

Generating Ideas

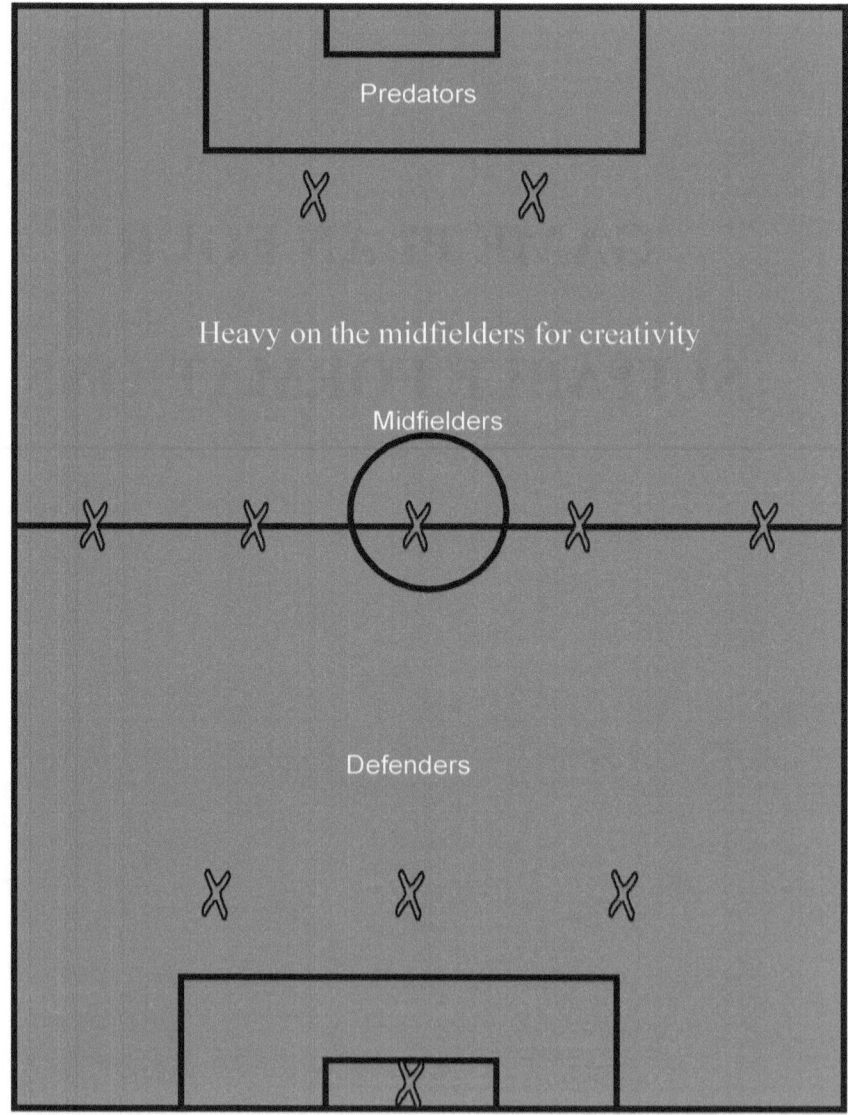

5-3-2

Working the idea

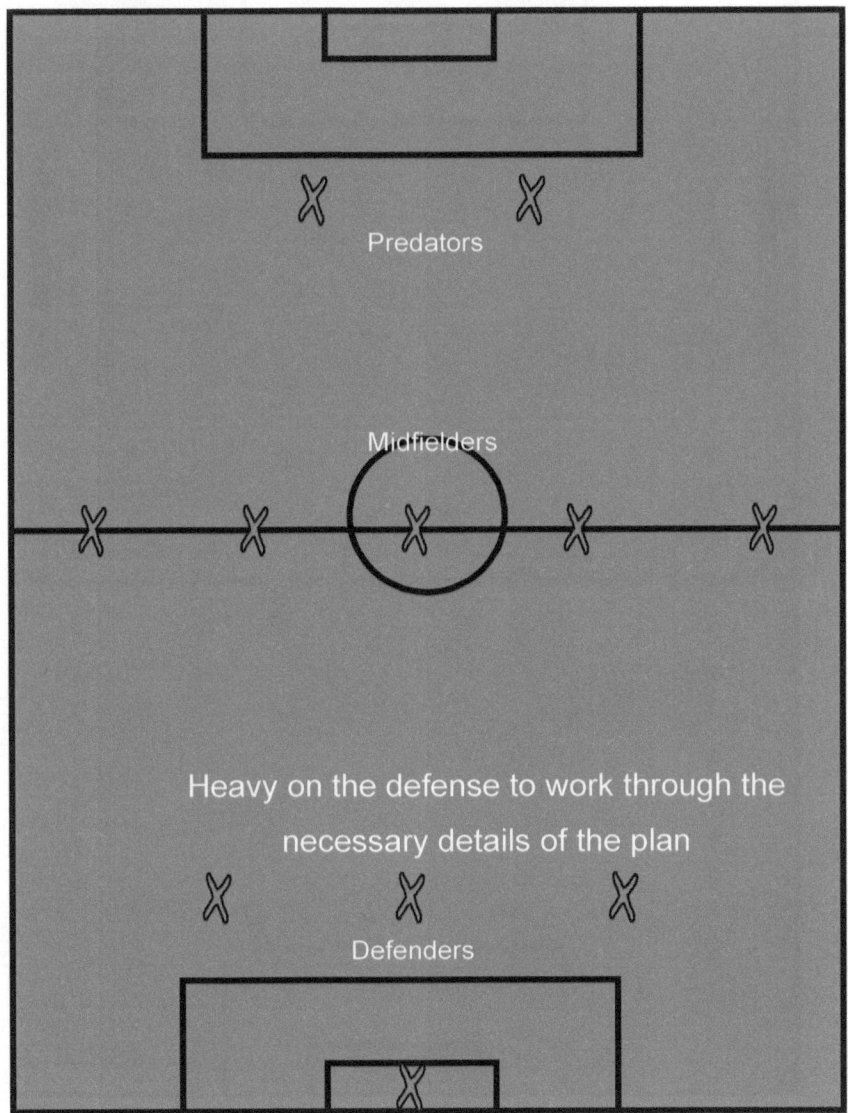

Predators

Midfielders

Heavy on the defense to work through the
necessary details of the plan

Defenders

4-2-4

Delivering the plan

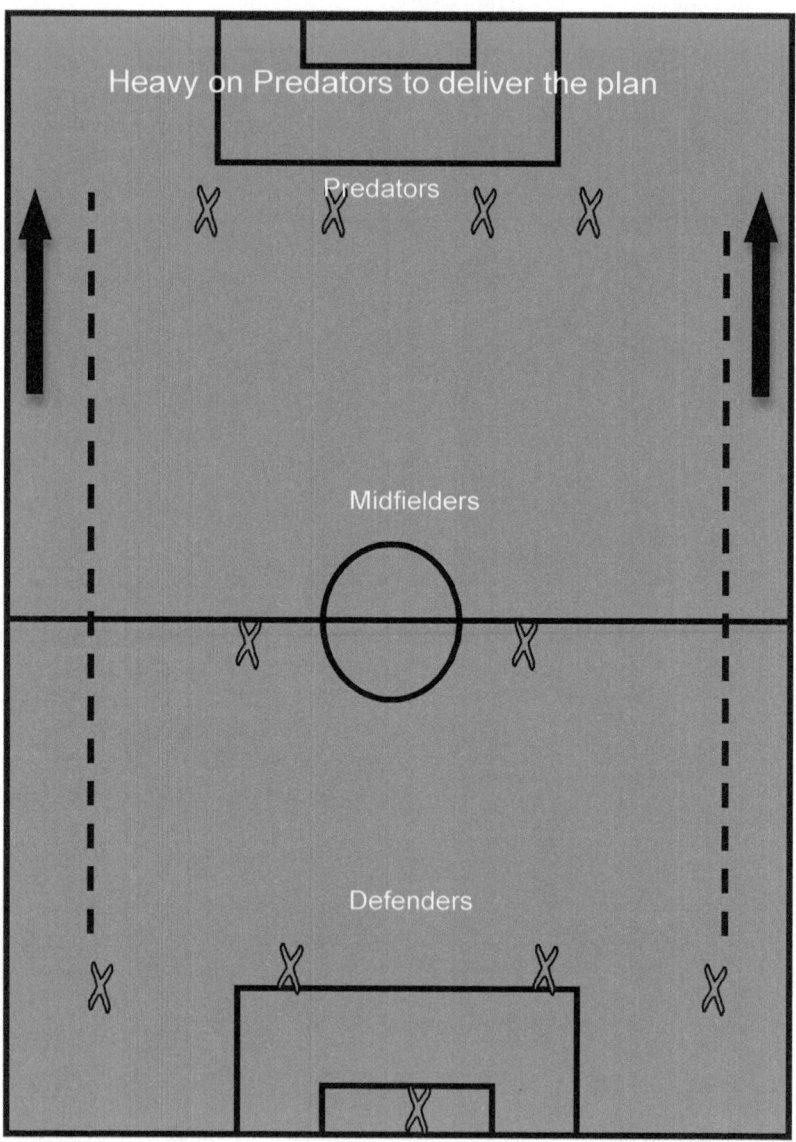

Just as in a game of soccer (or "football" for the purists), you have to know your opposition. How successful can a soccer team be if they know very little about the team they are trying to defeat? If you hope to win, you have to figure out the following:

The other team's reputation — are they aggressive, or do they go for skill versus brawn?

- Do they play a long ball and hope for the best?

- How much are they willing to spend on talent?

- Are they patient in their approach?

- How do they make decisions — quickly or slowly?

- Which formation have they used when they have played at their best?

- Who are their best players, and in what positions do they play their best?

- How is morale?

- What is their recent form? The list goes on, and a similar list applies to your business:

- How has the competition gone about their business?

- Are they aggressive?

- Are they selective in where and how they deliver?

- Do they make decisions quickly, or are they slow and more detail-orientated or traditional?

- Are they likely to turn down business that does not fit in with their mission statement? Or are they of the mindset that any moving target is fair game?

- How quickly have they grown? Has their growth surpassed their ability to keep up?

- What are their strengths and weaknesses as an organization?

- Who are their best people and where in the organization do they work?

- How many layers of decision-makers do they have (are they lean or fat)?

- How is morale?

Once you know all of this, you have to decide how you are going to play your game, what players you are going to need when you go head-to-head with that competition, and what formation you require. Do you need an aggressive group of managers with lots of stamina that will stay all the hours God sends, or creative teams that will out think the opposition? Do you need a nimble team that can move quickly and adapt to change to achieve results?

The answers to these questions will help you determine who you need to have on your team. Remember, you can have a great group of managers in your organization but if you play them out of place, they are likely to be average, at best. But if they play in a position where you know they are talented, you have yourself a well-balanced team that stands a realistic chance of winning the game. But, just like the soccer coach, you have to know your players! Once you have understood your competition and have established the skills of your own team, it is incumbent upon you to make sure you control the game and play to your strengths. In the next game plan, we will spend time learning how you can play to your strengths.

GAME PLAN FIVE

PLAYING TO YOUR STRENGTHS

Just as in any team sport, when an otherwise good employee is played out of position, the result is often a performance below expectations. However, the decision to fire an employee takes a fraction of the time it took to find them in the first place. When the day comes for the under-performer to be terminated, how many managers actually take time to consider where it all went wrong —from the employee's point of view? Probably very few.

In sports, without a proper assessment, a player not playing well is frowned upon. You blame them for doing a lousy job of passing the ball or for failing to see a potential danger that ultimately resulted in the team becoming vulnerable, when the reality is that maybe you were just playing them out of position. Here are some possibilities; maybe playing that person on the right side of the field is a poor decision because he or she is a left-footed player. Maybe giving a player two days to deliver better controls (for example, the Action Trigger, a predator) is difficult because they typically need more time to assess a situation before being able to understand how it all works (like an Anchor — a defender). Perhaps they are not doing well in a position requiring consistent, routine procedures because they have a passion for improving things and looking for better, more exciting ways of getting the job done (like the Idea Talisman — a midfielder). Placing a predator on defense is likely to result in them feeling ostracized from their peers, because they are not viewed as "team players" when the only reason is that they are bored with the role and not suited to the tasks. Here's the ironic thing: you put them there! And now you are blaming them. Before now, your only recourse was to tell them to work harder. Perhaps you have sent them on another training course because HR has told you to give them every opportunity to be successful. So off they go to training, but behavior doesn't change. You have no other recourse but to declare they are just underperforming and your department is suffering. Depending on the company culture, that person will then be moved to another area or fired. What a loss! Rarely does your organization come back to the hiring manager in an effort to try and figure out what went wrong during the hiring process, and how such a bad hiring decision could have been made. And if it wasn't you who made the decision to employ that person, you are not likely to be held accountable for losing talent unless you make a habit of it. Sometimes, without a doubt, a player may be very good, and may bring an immense amount of experience to your team. You may have been impressed by her years of experience in working with the products you are selling, or plan to sell in the near future. He may be the greatest innovator in your industry, or the most highly thought-of thinker in the country, but if your team is already strong in that area, then all you have done is improved your bench strength. Which may be fine if that was your intent. The timing may be completely wrong for them to join your organization. No doubt a good managerial decision, but the team you place on the field of play is not necessarily better for that recruitment decision unless there is an injury, like an unexpected absence or resignation. For example, if you have a team that is strong in the predator area but weak in defense, recruiting another predator is an ineffective use of your limited resources. He or she may be a great player, but you don't need him or her, and they are unlikely to improve the team at the time.

By understanding where your team is strong, you can play to those strengths. If you profile your team and the findings indicate that you have a strong group of predators, then play to that strength — predators are decisive and accurate. They can win games for you. Don't clutter up your team with lots of rules and bureaucratic procedures that will frustrate your players. The systems you have in place must reflect your team's strengths. Your procedures and methods, in a case like this one, have to reflect the way your team works best. A team that is full of good predators has the ability to be agile and, therefore a danger to your competitors; but hold them back with policies and you defeat yourself. When it comes time to recruit new players, don't just look for work experience, ask the right questions (see Game Plan 7). This will uncover their favored position on your team. Never mind that they have a strong marketing background, does your team need a defender, a midfielder, or a predator? Obviously, the experience the applicant brings with him is important, but only look at work experience at your peril. You may already be in the habit of looking for a personality that blends well with your team. However, the success of your team is not only dependent on each member's experience, or how funny, amiable, or kind they appear to be; it also lies in its ability to create synergy. You remember what that is? It's a group of individuals, each bringing a different set of skills that complement each other's strengths and weaknesses. Synergy creates fresh approaches, thereby surprising the competition of the day.

You, as the manager, also play on this team. But how do you decide which position is right for you? Profile yourself so you understand your behavior style, but don't let that confuse you about which position you should play in. In the next game plan, I will explain where you play in this formidable team you are creating.

GAME PLAN SIX

YOU'RE THE BOSS — WHERE DO YOU PLAY?

If you lead a team, you are the goalkeeper for every single game. The reason for this is quite simple — in this position you become the final defender of the company values. Isn't that part of your job, anyway? If the rest of the team is unable to stop the opposition making ground and threatening the company's security or market share, you become the final obstacle to losing the game. You have to be in the one position where you can see the entire field of play, give the team hope, and deny the opposition a winning opportunity if your team is vulnerable. And all this without having to be in the thick of the action all of the time. I once worked in what still is, in my opinion, Europe's best food retail company. We used to have a saying: "Nobody wants a manager that spends all of his or her time with their head stuck in a fixture." That meant if you are so caught up in the day-to-day running of your business — working in the business — then you are not in a position to be thinking and working on the business. It is your ability to water your organization's garden that makes it grow; just digging around in the weeds in one area will leave another part neglected.

You will have noticed, by now, two things about this position: The boss is the goalkeeper regardless of their profile. If any personality type can go in goal, the team will have to adjust the way it competes. It may change the way the defense organizes itself.

Let me explain point two, above, a little more: It becomes vitally important for the rest of the team to understand how to compensate for the goalkeeper (or team leader's) weaknesses. In any game of soccer, if the defense makes an assumption that the goalkeeper will be fast off the line, and he or she isn't, you'll have a situation where conceding a goal could be a near certainty. But if the defense is confident that the goalkeeper can jump high and pluck the ball away from danger, and he or she can, the defense only has to worry about the ground balls. Either way, the defense has to know when, and under what circumstances, their goalkeeper is at his or her best.

In the workplace, this is an interesting need-to-know concept. If the goalkeeper's profile puts them in the midfield, then, like the other members of that group, they are at their best dreaming up new ways to get things done. This is not the profile of a great defender; therefore, the defense with which he or she surrounds him or herself will have to be able to compensate for the fact that the team does have a great boss, but may be a little unpredictable at times.

Interestingly, you sometimes find a goalkeeper who has a tendency to go walkabouts. Although this can confuse the opposition and create entertainment for the neutral spectator, at the same time, it can also have the same confusing effect on the defense. The goalkeeper must be predictable for the sake of the team. The team, particularly the defense, must know what their goalkeeper is likely to do when danger lurks. It is when the defense is unclear what the manager, or goalkeeper, is going to do that they get a little jittery, and an irrational decision, under pressure, could result in an injury or, a goal! Your team must know what your profile is and where, if you were not the boss, it would place you on the field of play. I suppose there may be some who would feel having employees know you so well could leave you feeling a little naked or transparent, but this does not make you vulnerable! However, it does put your defense in a situation where their chances are better of guessing what you might do when the pressure is on, or how you might naturally think a problem should be handled and thereby understanding your paradigms better.

Let's explore this a little further with some examples. Suppose you, as the goalkeeper, have the profile that, given the choice, would operate much more comfortably in the midfield (see Game Plan Three). What happens when you (as the boss) decide you want your team to devise a new customer-service information system? As the creative thinker that you are, you will likely begin those creative juices flowing and look for a solution that is both sexy (meaning fun for you) and novel. If your team is aware of this, your defenders will ensure that the obvious solutions are not missed, and that your ideas are grounded and workable. That is the job of a good defense. However, if your team did not expect you to think this way, time would definitely be wasted as some of your players would discuss, by the coffee machine, what planet you are on. What tends to happen, in this case, is that your team will stand around waiting for you to critique their ideas and give them the direction they should focus on, and the details they must follow. Unfortunately, they are going to be waiting for a very long time! This is because you either do not find their ideas much fun, or you are off on the next adventure.

Have you ever seen the movie Big, with Tom Hanks? That's just how I envision a midfield executive. I don't mean to say that the midfield goalkeeper is immature or childish. But you must remember that it is the thrill of the unexplored that gets a midfielder's juices flowing, not the thrill of working out the details. If you don't remember, go back to Game Plan Three and re-familiarize yourself with the personality types of each of the three areas of the team. This is why it is so important that the midfielder, or predator, goalkeeper understands where his or her preferred position in the team would be if he or she were not the boss. It is necessary to make sure that the defenders employed also understand they will have a bigger role in working through the details with great accuracy before presenting the plan to you. If you are a natural predator you will get frustrated having to check so much detail; you'll do it because of your sense of duty, but it will be painful. And chances are you are going to pass it on to someone else to do the most excruciating details, anyway. However, if you are a midfielder, you will probably approach it from the standpoint of making the plan bigger or fancier (which ought to be someone else's job) rather than looking for ways the idea presented can work.

We have looked at the opposition, we have looked at your team, and now we have looked at you as the boss, where you will always play in the team, and how to ensure that you have the right people around you to complement your style. Now we are ready to play the game.

GAME PLAN SEVEN

PLAYING THE GAME

For a team to be effective, each player has to be able to identify with the organization. And you, as the manager, have to understand the make-up of your team. Your employees must know how the role they perform for the company affects everyone else; they also have to understand each role in the rest of their team on the field of play in order for the team to function well. You cannot afford for any striker (for example, the field sales agent) not to have a complete knowledge of what the midfield (for example, marketing) is doing. They also have to understand the role the marketing department plays in supplying a ready product to them so they can finish the job — score (or make the sale)!

In order to achieve this, effective communication is crucial. It makes no difference if the organization is mechanistic (top- down, close supervision), or boundary-less (everyone is in charge) in nature, nobody wins in business on his or her own. Even a lone small business owner relies on suppliers and local authorities to help him meet the needs of his or her customers. They form a team, and whereas that small business owner is not necessarily going to pick all of those team members, he is in a team, nonetheless. The business owner must understand where the players fit in the team. It is no different for a manager new to a business. Perhaps he has just received a promotion to a new department, or perhaps she has just started a new job. It would be foolish to walk in on the first day and dismiss all of the staff. A team is already in place. Each team member's strengths and weaknesses have to be understood. Using this concept offers a quick overview of how they are likely to play.

It may be that, once you have identified what skill-set makes up the team you have inherited, you find you have a team of defenders. Remember them? They are the group of people that just forge ahead; they don't care for change, they work well as a unit, and will analyze things to death! Left alone, they will never get anything finished. If your organization needs steadying, having a team of defenders may not be a bad thing, but if it needs revitalizing and some fresh approaches are required — you've got problems! You must first determine if any of your team's profiles have an 'N' in them (like an ENTJ — the Chairperson). It is likely someone does. Use one of them in the short term until you can find someone to permanently fill the role of a creator of ideas. This person is comfortable generating ideas, and is happy working outside the normal company practices (the midfielder). It's possible he or she might develop nicely into a midfield position on a permanent basis; nevertheless, using their skills will give you some breathing room while you work to find the right blend. The Chairperson could easily be your person to generate ideas for a period of time, but he or she would get restless after a while if that were the only thing you needed from them, because in the case of the Chairperson, they are not given the authority to mobilize the troops.

Suppose you have inherited a team of predators — a department practically full of doers that just want to get on with the job. It doesn't matter if the plan is poor, or the chances of any success are limited — they just want to get on with it. You will have to work alongside these people to get to get them talking. Bring them in the office for an armchair discussion and it won't be long before you've lost them. They'll be thinking about what they have to do when your meeting is over. And when it is over, you'll be left wondering if they listened to a word you said, or you might even be thinking they just don't seem to care. For their part, they may leave feeling the meeting was far too long, leaving them playing catch-up. To communicate effectively with this group you must learn to walk and talk. Go to their work environment and work alongside them. Sure, they might test you to see if you can keep up with them, but that's OK; it's not a gauntlet being thrown down — it's fun!

Early in my career, I worked in a location where the general manager was a predator. My first meeting with him was racing around his store. He literally ran up the stairs, I believe, to see if I could keep up. He wanted to know if I "had what it takes." He told me everything I needed to know about my new position in his store. But I will now admit I was worn out by the end of the day. I did not have to beat him to each destination as we tore around the place; I merely had to get there with him. I slept exceptionally well that night!

Sometimes, as with any team sport, the people you would like to have on your team just aren't available. It could be that they are just not on your payroll, or that they are absent for one reason or another. What do you do? Typically, you would shuffle the work around, or just leave it, depending on how long the person on your payroll is going to be gone. One or two days is not going to put you too far behind, in most circumstances, but what if they have a two- or three-week vacation? What if they are absent for some other reason for an extended period of time? It's for these situations that you have to prepare. It is at times like this that you have to know what you are going to do. Deciding what to do only when you are faced with the problem is a little late.

Even if you haven't prepared for an absence, knowing which people on your team are your defenders, your midfielders, and your predators, is going to be important. Imagine you have a project that your team has split up amongst them, with each person having a different assignment; in the worst-case scenario, you won't know where an absent person is on a particular project. After finding out from others working on the same thing, you could then bring in a midfielder to brainstorm how you can get the project finished on time and with the same expected quality. Without knowing who your midfielders are, you will likely bring in your closest associate, and if that person is a defender, and you're trying to brainstorm with them, you're going to be there all day! When any idea is placed on the board, all the brainstorming rules will go out of the window. This defender, an associate of yours, will analyze each one as it is placed on the board. Sure, you could explain to them that you're going to just write up the ideas and analyze them later, but as each one leaves your pen, they will not be able to help themselves making comments and extolling the virtues and highlighting the vices of each one. And in the end, it's a safe bet that you are going to be the one to come up with the workable solutions, anyway. Instead, knowing where your people fit on your team will enable you able to do the following:

1. Bring in a true midfielder and brainstorm for 15 minutes.

2. Then bring in one or two defenders, pick your plan to pieces, and come up with a finalized map.

3. And then, finally, give it to the most suitable predator to see if they could deliver.

Multi-tasking

If they are good, your team members can be relied upon to help in a time of crisis for short periods of time in any position. Some of them might probably do a pretty good job, too. But if you are going to be adequately covered, you must pick your slower times, or the not-so-important games, or practice sessions, to move your players around a little.

In the world of soccer, there are some outfield players who could also play well in the role of goalkeeper, and there are others who could be natural defenders for one game, wing-backs (see the 4-2-4 strategy in Game Plan Four) for another, or a midfielder, or even an out-and-out predator. But they are at their best when in their preferred positions. Here they can be creative within the safety their position allows. If you talk to some defenders, they will tell you they are very creative, and they undoubtedly are; however, everyone can be creative when measured against their team type.

A defender might consider herself creative when she has designed a new spreadsheet, and it could be very creative, but you wouldn't be rushing to have that person work on solving all of your customers' needs on the strength of that accomplishment!

As I mentioned before, everyone is creative, but to different levels. You cannot assume that, because someone has done something creative within the parameters of his or her job function, that he or she is a creative person in every sense of the word. Making these sorts of assumptions is how people get put in positions in which they ultimately fail. And when that happens, all eyes are on the person who is struggling. This is when the usual gravediggers come out, expressing how they always knew that person was the wrong one for the job, and in a sense, imitate the Queen of Hearts: "Off with their head!" Too few organizations point the finger at the hiring manager who failed to make them successful. That is, of course, unless that manager's boss wants to get rid of him or her, then the list of everyone's name that has become lost to the organization will get taken out of the drawer and used to slap the manager.

So when you first step in the door, profile your team, place them on the field of play, which you will have placed prominently on your wall, and thereby, prepare for the unseen. This will also help when you are recruiting. If you have positions you feel you are somewhat light on, then as you interview, look not only for the experience and skill-set that the new job-holder must have, but also ask questions that will identify how they will fit into your team.

For example, if you're looking for another predator, questions like:

1. "Tell me about a time you had to meet some difficult tasks." The answer may be "I kept at it until it was complete." In this situation, the candidate will want you to know that they will finish any task in front of them.

2. "How do you get things done?" The answer that may fit for this one is: "I have an ability to see problems quickly and fix them." Getting things done quickly is a source of pride for this type of player.

3. "What is your proudest moment?" For this one, a good

answer may be: "When my team/company became No.1 in the market." Everything is a competition for the predator, and they have to win.

If you are looking for a midfielder, your questions might include:

1. "Tell me about something you designed." For a question like this one, you will want to see an enthusiasm for creating new things.

2. "Tell me about a time you changed something the company traditionally did." Once again, it's about enthusiasm for encouraging change.

3. "What is your proudest moment?"

If you are looking for a defender, your questions might include:

1. "How long does it take to understand everything you need to know about a new job?" Time is important to a defender, they prefer to have the time to understand and they also feel a need to understand everything before they can move on.

2. "How would you approach a new task?" Here you're looking for details.

3. "How do you add value to any team?" Answers may

include things like "I make sure things are done right." Or "I do not let any detail escape me."

Obviously there are many more questions you could ask, but some like these will help you identify what type of player is in front of you.

In some circumstances, recruiting is not an option. This is always going to be the case when the cost of running the business is stretching the budgets to the limit. It is in times like this you have to multitask. Although thoroughbred midfielders are rare, as I mentioned before, some personality types are capable of doing a great job as stand-ins. Remember the key components to each area:

Defender

- Traditional

- Consistent

- Hard workers

- Good team players

- Resistant to change

Midfielder

- Creative.

- Energetic.

- Free-thinking.

- Unhindered by tradition.

- Might miss the obvious solution in favor of a more fun one.

Predator

- Decisive.

- Quick.

- Usually accurate.

- Pace-setters.

- Lone wolves.

There is always going to be some overlap with the personality types, simply because there are very few absolutes, so look for those things that will lend themselves to multi-tasking. For instance, you may be short of predators. If you have mostly defenders, you can place a defender in a situation where quick decisions are required. This will get them accustomed to making decisions on the fly rather than taking time to mull over every possible outcome before acting. As with every training exercise, don't let them just get on with it. If you do, they will fall back into what they do naturally, spend time on every detail, and may run out of room. In a soccer game, this might be when the ball is taken away from them by an unobserved opponent. You will have some defenders who can do that in certain circumstances, particularly if they are working in an area in which they are familiar. Similarly, if the employee is a predator, try placing him or her on a long-term project that has consequences sometime in the future, far enough away that they have the time to consider all of their options. In this sort of circumstance, they must have someone to report to who will keep them focused; otherwise, there is a danger they will take their eye off the ball for some immediate issues that may distract them, leaving the project you have assigned them to a later day.

Finding someone who can work in a midfield role is a little trickier. Although easy for a player natural to this area of the team, it can be a scary prospect for someone used to a more traditional approach. For such people as this, asking them to work in a world of uncertainty, and with abstract ideas, rather than practicality is daunting. However, as I mentioned earlier, those with the 'N' in their type are going to lend themselves more to this area. Get them to go out and learn what the competition is up to. They can gather the ideas they like, and think will work, use a defender's skill to analyze what has worked for the competition and what hasn't. Consider which of those practices would work in your organization's culture and then brainstorm a way to make the best solutions fit.

In conclusion, you will not always have the luxury of starting your team from scratch. More often than not, you are going to be appointed to lead a team of existing players. That is generally a good thing because you cannot place too high a value on experience; however, you must look to ensure that your team is balanced and take the corrective action if it is not. You will be able to place good players in unfamiliar positions for short periods of time, which will give you time to train and move players into their best positions for the long run.

Now you have your team in place and have identified where they can contribute to the best of their ability, you are now ready to look to the future. In the next Game Plan, you will find how this approach to teamwork can be used to build your next generation of leaders.

GAME PLAN EIGHT

THE YOUTH ACADEMY

Any team that focuses solely on the current first team is in danger of making themselves extinct in time. It is when a team is doing well that good people must be sought who will strengthen the current squad and provide quality individuals for the future. And it is when these young stars of the future are blended with experienced heads, in a kind of mentoring role, that the balance of the team remains intact and the future takes care of itself. Interestingly, in the world of soccer, the future of the team is placed in the hands of a youth team coach. In business, few organizations focus solely on the future talent by providing a youth team coach; however, what does happen is that attention and resources are spent on the current crop of players (managers) in the first team. Training programs are provided in an effort to improve their techniques and skills with whatever is left, going to some sort of college recruitment campaign or some other type of youth program. The problem with this is that, one day, those managers are going to reach their potential. Then what? You fire them, or you take it personally when they resign. For this to be effective, the management must be clear on what the future looks like for the organization. If they always play the same formation for every game, eventually the opposition will learn to second - guess them and neutralize their ability to be effective in the market place. Relate this to business and what I am saying is, if your level of service, or the products you supply, never change, then you open the door for your competition to leave you behind.

And so, the successful manager must become somewhat of a seer — accurately forecasting the market's needs and how his or her team will have to evolve to remain competitive.

Recruiting a manager who will help your company do what it already does well, or is currently doing, is a mistake with potentially fatal consequences.

Once the future has been predicted, the players who will achieve that end must be identified — not necessarily by name, but certainly by skill-set. For example, suppose you expect to keep your current set of customers over a period of time. As they get older, it is likely that their preferences will change with age and, like a good wine, "mature." Alternatively, if your company sells a product that appeals to a younger age group, then it is obvious that you are going to be dealing with a whole set of new customers in a few years if you are planning to remain the company of choice to that age group. Your team of the future will have to be able to address those needs, so what are you looking for? What shape, what formation, and what skill-set will you need? This is where the Youth Academy applies. Not only must they be fully immersed in the company culture, they must be better than the market average in whatever it is they are employed to do in the future. This may mean that they are not the individuals who can offer you much today, but they are handpicked for tomorrow, knowing that the game plan will have changed when it is their time to turn on the style on the field of play.

Obviously, the Youth Academy has no reference to age; rather it is your training ground for the next generation of managers within your organization. They are either your purchased talent for the future, or internal talent that has been identified as having the ability, with specific training, to lead your organization into the future.

Have you ever sat in a room where the discussion was on succession planning? You may be working for one of the better companies that has a living plan that is up-to-date and accurately identifies the organization's talent. However, I suspect many of you work for a company that, if they have one, the plan is an inside joke. Names are placed on a list to satisfy higher-ups in the company that everyone is living up to the expectation that people are being developed. Although some of the better companies in this class schedule regular meetings to discuss each of these individuals, when they are actually needed, here come the barriers:

- "They need about six months more." To do what?

- "Their circumstances have changed and they are now unwilling to relocate." Oh really! Or is it that you are just trying to protect your own interests and fend off the wolves from other departments getting their hands on your top talent?

- "They need more people-management training." If they are incapable of managing people, how did they get on the plan in the first place?

- "Last year's ratings were very unrealistic." So how did it get past you?

- "This person will be ready for the beginning of next FISCAL." Really! They have been in the same job for 10 years, but finally they will be ready in a few months? And you know we all believe that one!

You can just hear the jokes that are shared as folks gather around the water cooler to discuss the "succession plan." Using this team approach, a detailed plan for an individual's development is tied directly to what the company will expect to be doing next, and what the anticipated people resource need will be. For example, perhaps the current market for your organization is changing and your current strength as an operations company will have to change. Maybe you will need to be more sales-focused, or marketing-intensive; perhaps you will be experiencing some retirement in key departments that will diminish your defender population. Now you must look to recruit people with a proven record in stick-to-it-iveness and analysis. Perhaps you have noticed that you have the same problem that Tom Kendall noticed in his team in the earlier metaphor, that you just do not have enough people to finish the tasks because so many people either have their heads in the clouds, or are spending so much time analyzing, that nobody is focusing on the execution.

Now your recruitment and development plans are tied directly into the organizational needs. Managers understand how they impact the business. They not only bring core competencies to the party, but they can also see how they add value to future business practices and projects, and their return on investment is for everyone to see.

Beware of those organizations that pat themselves on the back over the fact that they do not train talented individuals, they merely go out and buy the talent they need. Unwittingly, these companies provide a great opportunity for some other organization to take their place in the market, because each new player they purchase needs a ramp-up time. That time will vary, depending on the person, the complexity of the job, and the company culture, but these companies will be caught in a continuous ramp-up period that will create gaps in the organization's growth. By utilizing a Youth Academy effectively, you will not need to worry about the same settling period for your new appointees, and time is money.

Integrating fresh talent into the first team is an art. Move them in too fast and you may be setting them up for failure; take too long to give them a taste of first-team action and you may lose them. In the greatest soccer league in the world there are many examples of young talent being introduced to the big time slowly and methodically. There are also some sad examples of poor management forcing talent into the spotlight too early, and they have amounted to nothing, still talking about how great they are. Disillusioned, they spend the rest of their days trying to convince people they have talent. Managing this group of employees' expectations isn't easy. But once you have made the decision to introduce them to first-team action (promote them to a manager position) make sure you surround them with experienced heads to mentor them and keep them on course.

In the next chapter, we will look at the different applications of this model. Using this team approach can have as broad of applications as you want.

GAME PLAN NINE

OTHER APPLICATIONS

In this chapter, we consider other ways to use this team concept to your advantage. Morale will improve as each manager becomes a go-to person at the different stages of this game we call "work."

As team sheets are published (or organization charts, but not set out like all the others you are used to seeing: with a manager at the top and everyone else below and with solid and dotted lines all over the place. I am talking about a team sheet laid out like the ones you have seen earlier in this book with your people's names on) everyone will know who to go to for support (even the water-cooler crowd.) The sheet may look like this:

Team Model

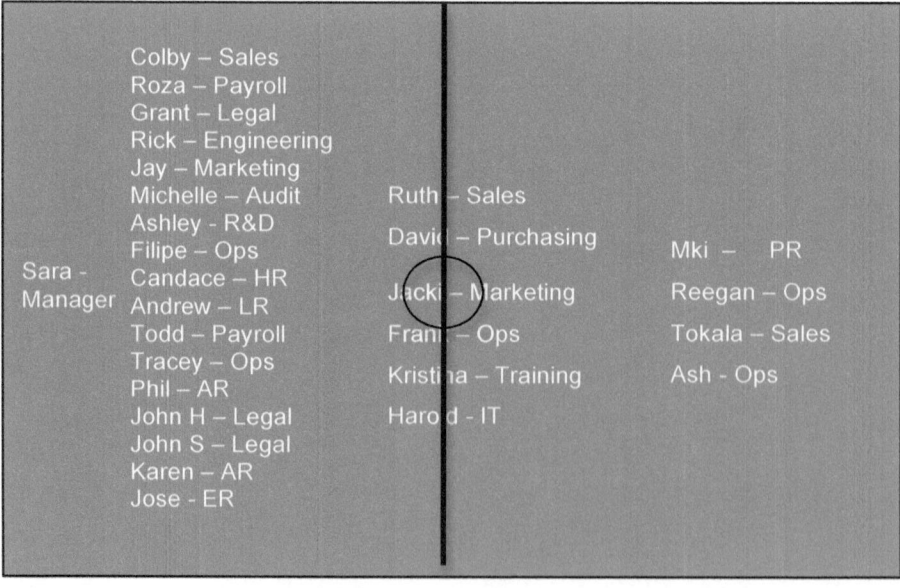

Your team may not look like this one in terms of balance, but you get the picture. Incidentally, Do you see any issues with how the departments are represented? If, after you have profiled your team, departments are heavily represented by one area of the team, that may be a problem. Keep reading to understand why, but do not misunderstand the point of this idea. Each player has a job to do; profiling them will help you, as the manager, comprehend how they are going to approach their job. None of these people are just hanging around, waiting for the next project to come along — like spare parts. Neither are they a separate group. They are all employed to work in a department and used for special tasks, as needed. They are individuals you can turn to for a more balanced team for project-working purposes, or just for help with a one-off need.

What if you had an important presentation to do next week? Why not give it to a defender and ask him or her to analyze it and give you some detailed feedback? If it comes back with a mass of red notations all over it, take it to a midfielder and ask them how it could be better, more original, or how you could improve the flow, or ask for some ideas on attention-getters. And just before you are ready to deliver it, check with a predator and see if they could see themselves delivering your idea.

Here are some more applications:

I. Mentoring

Trying to match people with a mentor is no easy task. When doing so, you may consider some of the following:

1. Does she have enough time?

2. Is he patient enough?

3. Does she know the job well enough?

4. Is the mentor accessible to the mentee?

5. Does he know enough about the job of the mentee?

6. Does she have the courage to be candid and honest in giving feedback?

These are all good questions. How about the person being mentored?

1. What is she to get out of it?

2. How will he be a better person, leader, or manager through the mentoring program?

3. Would she get along with the mentor?

4. What type of personality is required to offer the best form of feedback for this mentee?

As you use the team concept in this book, it becomes easy to discover which part of the team an individual should go to for them to benefit. You will find the company will have a better employee at the end of it (whether a mentor is used only by means of an introduction to the company, or for ongoing development, or both.) This is because new hires who have been profiled will fit into a particular part of the team. Let's consider a predator. Selecting a mentor from the same area, or from the midfield or defense, will give you differing and targeted results. Let's take a look at the three possible scenarios:

A predator with another predator as a mentor will help the new hire understand how his paradigms fit into the new organization's culture — valuable lessons to be taught.

Placing the same new hire with a midfielder will help her understand how creativity happens in the organization; it can also show the predator how ideas are conceived. This is good because a predator is not likely to spend much time in this area once she is established, unless it is for personal development, because it is not usually a comfortable place for her to be.

Finally, although placing the new hire with a defender may drive the predator crazy, this is a good way to help him understand that sometimes you just have to slow down and consider the details. This is another good way of establishing a long-term relationship, which can also occur with the midfielder or predator mentors.

If the new employee happens to be a midfielder (depending on the company and the needs of the department) it may be entirely appropriate to have another, company-experienced midfielder, to help them develop their skills, discover their natural abilities, and then deliver as an out-of-the-box thinker. In this case, the mentor could also teach the new employee how to make the best use of his or her natural style within the company culture.

However, pairing him or her with a defender will provide an opportunity for him or her to see how ideas are worked through. This will give him or her a wonderful chance to understand what is important to the organization and what sort of tests each idea must go through before it's adopted. You may decide that the person needs to have more exposure to someone who can give him or her a better foundation in the business.

It is easy to spot a defender and a midfielder, but predator skills are harder to notice. Using this concept of team development right from the start will help you identify each player's best position at an earlier stage (assuming they were honest with their answers).

Team Rotation

This is about strengthening your squad — multi-tasking. Traditionally, this is a one-sided solution to scheduling problems. Management will use the argument that if an employee knows how to do more jobs in the organization, the employee becomes more valuable. The reality is that once the employee knows the other jobs, he or she is sometimes wrenched from place to place, rarely having an opportunity to finish a task. But using this team concept, employees are developed not only in skill but in style, also. And as each employee finds his or her style and learns how to use it, everyone wins.

Next, we will look at each section of the team and discuss this concept in detail:

Defenders

Defenders like more time than any other player on the team when working on projects, and may be meticulous to the point of fault, preferring a more measured approach to tasks, and they are great team players. Suppose your team was short of predators, but heavy on defenders. Assuming recruitment was not an option, how would you go about the task of balancing your team? One way would be to place a defender in a number of short-term projects with a group of predators. This process would have to be monitored because, left alone, the defender might become frustrated at the lack of attention to detail his project teammates demonstrate. In the defender's mind, one should never take what others say as gospel; everything should be tested against set standards to make sure there are not any flaws. As the predators make a quick spot-check and then run off to deliver the plan, the defender would be the last one out of the door, still calling out after them "but we're not ready yet! What about...?" and if this continues, frustration and disillusionment are going to set in. In such a case, the defender will need someone to share his or her concerns with and be constantly reminded that, in this group, quick spot-checks are the order of the day, followed by deliverance of the plan to the team's satisfaction. At the same time, the rest of the members in this project team may need regular monitoring to ensure they are not getting frustrated at having a defender amongst them, because she is slowing them down and boring them with too many details! Imagine a room of predators, each with glazed-over eyes as the defender tries to impress them with details!

Suppose you wish to increase the number of midfielders, or just provide some development within your pool of defenders. This can be an interesting journey, particularly if you are trying to do this with a hard-core defender like an Anchor (ISFJ) or a Guardian (ISTJ). You will remember that placing some people in the world of possibilities and of abstract thinking may be an excruciating experience. To the hard-core defender, midfielders have their heads in the clouds. Some of them may also think midfielders rarely add value, because defenders see them as always being somewhere else concocting some other half- baked idea when they should be worried about getting the job done in the present — not worrying about the future. Some defenders may enjoy the idea of generating ideas but may spoil the party somewhat when a brainstorming session is in progress and they keep analyzing each idea as it is thought of — obviously not the idea behind brainstorming. With training, some defenders can do very well in a midfielder role; but you must remember, in order to avoid burnout, it is only a temporary solution, but one than can provide a significant development opportunity.

b. Midfielder

The midfielder is probably the hardest area of your team to develop into. For a defender to become one, it takes considerable courage to let go of those tried-and-tested procedures, methods, or systems. The predator would not find the unstructured approach of a creative teammate appealing, because dreaming up new ways of doing things is fine, but to a predator it is usually a waste of valuable time. What you may get from a defender is a variation on what you already do well, and that may be good enough, but if you need something completely new, don't rely on the ideas of a defender to deliver that. However, there are ways to do this effectively. The naturally analytical mind of the defender may be used to study what other companies are doing and consider how those things could be effectively adapted to your own business. This is called "conceptual thinking" (developing an existing idea). An example of conceptual thinking would be communication. Man has always communicated, even if only through grunts, but often not very well, even today. Improving on communication requires looking at better methods. If someone invents a better electronic method, that would be conceptual in terms of communication. You could go back to when the first phone was produced; it may have been unique at the time (innovative) but as a method of communication it was an improved way of doing something, we already did (conceptual). Going through the painstaking detail of "what ifs" would help a midfielder understand how the ideas they are making impact the workforce. Some midfielders have tremendous follow-through. Many are happier just to generate the ideas and then move on (when one is accepted) with nothing more than a general outline.

On the other hand, innovation (developing a never-before- thought-of idea) requires a greater degree of risk — and that does not come easily to many people. A good example of innovative thinking is the wheel. In ancient Mesopotamia, this solid circular construction made the creation of pottery easier. This was revolutionary at the time — and is an example of innovation. It became conceptual when someone got the idea to make it lighter by making spokes in the middle, cutting away some of the solid wood, and... voila! The wheeled cart appeared as a method of transportation.

Getting someone to become conceptual in thinking is a first step toward innovation because it cuts away some of the traditional thinking that can shackle an individual to the past. By introducing a defender to conceptual thinking and helping them develop their skills in this way, you will introduce the defender to the creative world of the midfielder.

Predator

Since the benefit for a predator may be to learn patience and teamwork, having them work on projects that require more detail and time to deliver would be a great asset for them. You have to understand the risk of doing this; they may turn people into nervous wrecks as they stand at the door tapping their feet in an attempt to hurry the team into action, demonstrating an obvious frustration with the time taken to get the job finished.

Some people really are natural at making quick decisions. People that are naturally very good at this are fascinating to watch. I have known some very quick and deadly accurate thinkers. One who will always stand out in my mind is a manager working in a food retail store in Europe. He just seemed to be able to make decisions with little delay. It was almost as if he could gather information, process it, and make a decision, all in one step. I truly admire this quality in a manager. However, this skill can be learned — predators do not own this skill, it just comes easier to them. Placing people in a position where quick decision-making is essential will ultimately achieve this.

As you follow this process you will encounter a balance rarely experienced except on those rare occasions when luck plays a significant part. There is no reason to leave the success of your team to luck, no reason to cross your fingers and hope the group will find synergy — you can create it. You can hire the right people, at the right time, in the right place, with the right style to balance your team and to provide the skills the job requires. And if the lack of funds impedes your ability to hire, now you know how to develop each player on your team so they will add value across the field of play — the market in which your company trades.

GAME PLAN TEN

BROADENING THE BRUSH

The method for measuring each player on this field of play has obviously come from a study of the book Please Understand Me: Character and Temperament Types, written by David Keirsey and Marilyn Bates. It is important that you know this book has not been produced with any endorsement from Meyer's-Briggs, nor from Keirsey and Bates. I am not a Meyer's-Briggs employee, and they are not getting paid one dime for any of the comments made herein. I applaud their work and take no credit away from them for the book they have produced. It is possible to identify your players' strengths and weaknesses, and where they may fit on the field of play (defense, midfield, or predator) without any kind of profile. You could take a look at the people who appear to be the most creative, and decide they must be your midfielders. You could also do the same by looking at your detailed people and calling them your defenders, or your quick studies and fast decision-makers as your predators; however, applying a personality profile like the one I have used in this book ensures a consistency of approach.

Teamwork is only a piece of a much larger pie because it is a slice of organizational efficiency. Effective teams are part of what will make your organization a productive, money-making machine each and every day you are in operation. Nobody is suggesting that having your players play in the right positions is all you need, but this book focuses on how much better you can operate when you play to your team's strengths.

The name of this book is YaGottaWanna: Winning Takes Teamwork. I believe that! If you lack the passion and will to win, or if you really don't want to win the game, then you won't. That may sound too simplistic, but if you have decided, or your boss has placed you in a position that is not allowing you to play to your strengths, then maybe that is the problem. And maybe the fact that you are not enjoying your job is down to that — not that you are employed with the wrong company. Perhaps you are just playing out of position. Perhaps your success is measured against your ability to get things done quickly (a predator) when you would rather take your time making sure every "i" is dotted, and every "t" is crossed (a defender). Armed with this information, you are in a better position to figure out how to play to your strengths. And then, when you have figured that out, you can then look at your team and consider if you have placed them in the best position that will give your company the best return on its investment.

The club directors (the stakeholders), and the fans (the other stakeholders) are willing you to do well. It is in their best interests that you do your best, and if you are playing out of position and lack the ability, or the desire, to play there, then this book is a must for you!

I wish you luck as you use this simple and visual method to get your team operating at peak performance, and maybe you and I will meet on the field of play one day.

BIBLIOGRAPHY

Gladwell, Malcolm. (2002). The tipping point: how little things can make a big difference. Little, Brown & Company.

Keirsey, David; Bates, Marilyn. (1984). Please understand me: character & temperament types. Gnosology Books Ltd.

Orwell, George. (1996). Animal farm. NAL

ABOUT THE AUTHOR

Malcolm Paice has been training managers for many years. His personable, energetic, and humorous style of teaching has given him plaudits from North America to Europe. Malcolm has a unique ability to connect with his audiences whether they are executives or hourly employees he generates an enthusiasm with his simple "how to" methods that consistently produce positive results. He is also a qualified soccer coach and referee.